10

ABSOLUTE
LIFE-CHANGERS
OF MEN;
GUARANTEED:

FROM THE BOOK WHICH CANNOT LIE

10 Absolute Life-Changers of Men; Guaranteed:
From the Book Which Cannot Lie
Copyright © 2009

All Rights Reserved.

ISBN-13: 9781935256021

Published by L'Edge Press
A ministry of Upside Down Ministries, Inc.
PO Box 2567
Boone, NC 28607

Dedication

For several years I have searched the Scriptures, researched the lives of godly men, and drawn from my own experience to find the 10 truths which transform men into the "image of Christ" (Romans 8:29). These 10 truths constitute the core of our curriculum in "Mentoring Men for the Master," and as men have obeyed these disciplines I have seen them become powerful "change agents" in their homes, churches, vocations, and world. It is to these men that I gratefully dedicate this book and to the growing number of men across the world who will yet be changed – all to the glory of God.

Deo Soli Gloria

Endorsement Of My Mentoring

Dr. Adrian Rogers: "Being mentored by Bill Bennett would be a blessing that no seminary can give."

Dr. Daniel Akin, President of Southeastern Baptist Theological Seminary: "Bill Bennett's passion for mentoring young men to be leaders in the work of the Lord is well known…He recognizes that this was the model of Jesus and it should be our model as well. His approach is biblical, practical and devotional."

Dr. David Black, Professor of New Testament and Greek, Southeastern Baptist Theological Seminary: "Bill Bennett is one of my closest friends. Together for a year we met weekly for prayer and mutual encouragement. I know of few men I would rather be mentored by."

Dr. Jerry Falwell: "I have known Bill Bennett for nearly 35 years. The passion of his soul for many years has been to build up young men in their ministries. He has done this most effectively through mentoring them…"

Dr. Allen Moseley, Professor, Southeastern Baptist Theological Seminary: "Bill Bennett knows how to mentor men. He has done it effectively for decades. And the proof is in the pudding – many men who are walking with God and faithfully serving God proudly refer to Dr. Bennett as their mentor."

Dr. Jimmy Draper, Former President of Lifeway Christian Ministries: "Bill Bennett has spent his life in relationships and mentoring. No one does it better than he."

Dr. Jim Henry: "The word 'mentor' was not on my radar in early years of ministry. But it was in the heart of Bill Bennett when the Holy Spirit placed him in my life during seminary days. Forty years later I continue to learn from him."

Terry Fox, Pastor, Summit Church, Wichita, Kansas, Former Chairman of NAMB: "I had the privilege of training under Dr. Bennett's leadership. His mentoring changed my personal life and ministry and I am still using the tools for mentoring he taught me."

Table of Contents

Chapter 1

Internalizing the Word

God clearly called me to preach in 1950, and this I did with a great joy and extraordinary results for 36 years. In 1986 God clearly called me to leave the pastorate and begin to mentor men as clearly as He called me to preach. However, He did not instruct me as to how I was to proceed in this task of mentoring, but simply said, "it would be the greatest ministry I had ever known."

I then began to search the Scriptures to discover what God had to say about mentoring. Then I discovered four fundamental facts relating to mentoring:

1. God's purpose for every child of His is for him to "be conformed to the image of Christ" (Romans 8:29) in order for him or her to become a true Christ-follower.

2. For one to be conformed to Christ's image he would need to discipline himself in specific activities. As the apostle Paul commanded, "Discipline yourself for the purpose of godliness" (1 Timothy 4:7b NASV).

3. Mentoring would include my "coming alongside" my students as well as teaching in class. My golden text is 1 Thess. 2:8 (NIV), "We loved you so much that we were delighted to share with you not only the gospel of God but our lives as well, because you had become so dear to us."

4. The specific disciplines required for "conforming to His Image" consisted of 10 imperatives clearly stated in the Scriptures. I spent considerable time in prayer and study before the Lord revealed these disciplines to me. I am not an incurable devotee to alliteration, but since I could clearly state each of these disciplines with a word beginning with the letter "I," I began to refer to them as "The 10 I's." Some clearer titles might be "The 10 Imperatives for Continuing

1

Spiritual Growth," "The 10 Life Changers," or "The 10 Steps to Becoming like Jesus," or "The Big 10 of the Kingdom." I finally settled on one title, which is "The 10 Absolute Life-Changers for Men – From the Book Which Cannot Lie."

1. Internalizing the Word – Joshua 1:8; James 1:18-25
2. Infilling of the Holy Spirit – Ephesians 5:18
3. Intimacy with the Father – Psalm 27:4
4. Intentional Involvement in the World Mission of Christ – Matthew 28:18-20
5. Interrelating with others to share your life – (Mentoring) – 1 Thess. 2:8
6. Investing your money redemptively with the Lord, beginning with the tithe to your local church – Matthew 6:19-20
7. Identification with, support of, and service in a local church – Hebrews 10:25
8. Intense devotion to one's family, especially his wife – Eph. 5:25; 1 Peter 3:7.
9. Intentional discipline of the physical body – 1 Cor. 9:27; Romans 12:1
10. Instant repentance and cleansing from all sin – Psalm 139:23-24.

We meet with our mentorees weekly to instruct them in the nature and practice of these 10 disciplines, and we also "come alongside" them during the week both to encourage them to obey these activities and to hold them accountable in so doing. As men have submitted themselves to these biblical teachings, we have witnessed phenomenal changes for the better in both their attitudes and actions. To be more specific, men who had been "wimps" have become godly husbands to their wives, wonderful fathers and examples to their children, faithful and effective church members, and outstanding Christian citizens. The wives of our mentorees are often saying to me, "Dr. Bennett, I don't know what you are doing in mentoring my husband; but whatever it is, please keep on doing it, for it has given me a new man."

With this background I will now list the 10 I's, define each one, and give supporting Scripture and collateral materials to further amplify their full meaning:

1. **The Internalization of the Word of God.** The Bible clearly commands us to take several actions concerning the Word of God:
   a. Read the Word (1 Timothy 4:13)
   b. Study the Word (2 Timothy 2:15)
   c. Search the Word (Acts 17:11)
   d. Desire the Word (2 Peter 2:2)
   e. Love the Word (Psalm 119:97)
   f. Treasure the Word (Job 23:12)
   g. Hide the Word (Psalm 119:11)

But the Bible commands far more than any of these things. The Bible commands us to "Internalize the Word," or to "eat" the Word (Jeremiah 15:16; Ezekiel 3:1; Revelation 10:9) until we "abide" in the Word or literally find nourishment for our souls and day-by-day guidance for our lives. In fact the very essence of our lives becomes the Word of God. As Jesus said, "Man shall not live by bread alone but by *every word* which is proceeding out of the mouth of God" (Matthew 4:4). Moreover, He asserted that the mark of the true disciple is abiding or internalizing the Word. "If you abide in my Word, you are my disciples indeed and you shall know the truth and the truth shall make you free" – John 8:31-32. Faithful believers read and even study the Word, and many hear the Word and even preach and teach it without ever "Internalizing" the Word.

Thus the Lord showed me that the "Internalization" of the Word consist of 4 steps. These steps are the heart of our "Mentoring curriculum," and so very important that we have incorporated them into our "Bible Pledge," which goes as follows: With everyone standing, holding his Bible in his right hand, we repeat together this pledge:

"This is my Bible. It is God's inerrant word. It is my most valuable earthly possession. I will, therefore, make it a lamp unto my feet and a light unto my path and I will hide its words in my heart that I might not sin against God.

The Bible is God talking to me personally. I will, therefore, listen to it carefully and obey it fully. I will endeavor to internalize it in my life by doing 4 things:

1. I will *Know* it in my head by diligent *study.*
2. I will *Stow* it in my heart by *memorization and meditation,*
3. I will *Show* it in my life by *obeying* its teachings,
4. I will then *Sow* it into my world by witnessing.

Hereafter I will never be the same, never, never, never, in the name of Jesus and for His honor and glory both now and forever. Amen"

When we can truly offer the "Bible Pledge," we can joyfully repeat the "Victory Pledge," as follows:

"I am too anointed to be disappointed,
I am too blessed to be depressed,
I am too chosen to be frozen,
I am too elected to be rejected,
I am too inspired to be tired,
Have more to shout about
Than to pout about, And have more to sing about
Than complain about."

Our first lesson in Mentoring consists of "Internalizing" the 10 Commandments and the 8 Beatitudes. For example, take the 10 Commandments:

First, we ask our students to memorize each commandment (first step).

Secondly, we ask our students to "meditate" on the commandments until they understand their meaning and how each would apply to their individual lives (second step).

Thirdly, we ask our students to explain how they would keep this commandment in every day living (third step).

Fourthly, we ask our students to explain how they would use this truth in witnessing, teaching, preaching, telephoning (fourth step).

We go a step further and demonstrate by the acrostic FIRST what it means to "Internalize" the 1st commandment of the 10: First, we point out that the first commandment in plain language means "You shall put God first in every area of your life:"

F – in your **Finances** – Tithe to your local church, give offerings and use the rest for His glory.

I – in your **Interests** – show He is Lord over every aspect of your life.

R – in your **Relationships** – He is Lord over your relationships to everyone.

S – in your **Schedule** – put the Lord first.

T – in your **Time** – spend your time to do all He commands in His Word.

We continue to demonstrate how to internalize the remaining nine "I's" – these principles are applied to all the Scriptures.

The results: Most of our students have read the Bible, some have even memorized portions, before they come to our Mentoring School, but they had never gone on to "meditate" on it, understand its deep meaning, and how it applied to their everyday lives. One guy was brought up in an Independent Baptist Church where great emphasis was laid just upon memorizing the Bible, but nothing else. This brother began to follow our 4 steps in "Internalizing" the Word and exclaimed, "Up until now I thought there was something "magic" just in being able to quote the Word, but now I see that the real change comes when I "Internalize" the Word instead.

Conclusion: The Word of God will change any life but only if it gets on the "inside" of a person, and the word gets on the "inside" only when one internalizes it When it does, the Holy Spirit takes that Word and changes one's mind and behavior and he begins to conform into the image of Christ, making him a godly Christian, husband, father, church member – a true Christ-follower.

Permit me then to make it crystal clear that Bill Bennett nor has anyone else ever changed anyone, but the Holy Spirit, using the word on the "inside," has and is changing hundreds of men across the earth and to Him be all the honor and glory. My guiding word is Isaiah 42:8, "I am the Lord; this is my name, and I will not share my glory with another…" God forbid that I do.

Collateral Material On The First "I"
Dangers To Avoid In "Internalizing The Word"

1. **Legalism** – Legalism would be seeking to Internalize the Word as a mere duty, void of love for Jesus and dependence upon the Holy Spirit.

2. **Ritualism** – Ritualism is a customarily repeated, often formal act or series of acts (Webster's) Thus ritualism is organized "legalism," requiring no heart or love but mere adherence to a prescribed procedure.

3. **Meritorious Righteousness** – Some may "Internalize the Word," believing the more they do so, the more righteous they become in the eyes of God and man. Such activity only builds our pride and rather than enhancing our relationship with God, it prevents it. Remember, "God resists the proud, but gives grace to the humble" – 1 Peter 5:6.

4. **Partial Internalization** – There are four steps in "Internalizing the Word." Satan would smile to see you memorize verses, but never really meditate on them, never applying them to one's life, and never sharing them. James warns "Be not hearers of the Word but doers, deceiving yourself" – James 1:22.

How do you know if you are falling into one of these dangers? Simply this way: If you are finding no joy, but only constant struggle, dread, and desire to stop, in all probability it is because you are approaching Internalizing as a legalistic duty, a ritualistic habit without heart, an act to make you more righteous, or you are only partially meeting the four requirements for internalization.

Interpret all Scriptures according to its contextual setting. Otherwise you stand in danger of completely falsifying the Scriptures and teaching plain error.

Example # 1 – "The Bible says that if you confess your sins you will be saved." False

"It really says, "If we confess our sins, He is faithful and just to forgive us our sins" (1 John 1:9). These familiar words are often quoted as a formula for salvation. But the presence of the word "we" in the immediate context makes it clear that John was not addressing the unsaved. Rather, he was talking to people who were already believers in Christ (vv. 6,7,9,10), and was showing them how to be restored to a right family relationship with the God who had saved them. If we don't consider the immediate context, we might conclude that we are saved by admitting our sins rather than by believing the gospel of Christ."[1]

Example # 2 – "The Bible says that it's wrong for a woman to wear jewelry?" False

"The actual quote is : 'Do not let your adornment be merely outward – arranging the hair, wearing gold, or putting on fine apparel' (1 Peter 3:3). Some have used these words to say that godly women should not style their hair, use cosmetics, or wear jewelry. But if we read on, we find these words, "rather let it be the hidden person of the heart" (v. 4). By these additional words we see that the apostle's main purpose was not to tell women that they either should or should not style their hair or wear jewelry. He was saying that they should focus on the beauty of a gentle and quiet spirit rather than relying on outward appearance."[2]

Example #3 – "The Bible says that studying for knowledge isn't necessary." False

"It actually says, 'If any of you lacks wisdom, let him ask of God, who gives to all liberally and without reproach, and it will be given to him (Jas. 1:5). These words of James have been seen by some as a promise that

---

[1] Martin De Hann II, *How Can I Understand the Bible*, Grand Rapids, Michigan: Discovery House Publishers, 2003, p. 9.
[2] Ibid. p. 9

7

we can receive unlearned skills and knowledge if we just pray. More than a few college students have claimed this promise before taking an exam for which they had not prepared.

The immediate context, however, is describing a reason for the joy we can have when difficult circumstances test our faith. James' promise is not that we can be successful without effort, but rather that God does not leave us alone when He allows trouble or temptation to come into our lives. James assured us that if we don't know how to let God do His work in us, we can have wisdom for the asking.

Later in the same letter, James told his readers how to recognize this wisdom when it comes. He said it is not marked by envy or selfish ambition, but is 'pure, then peaceable, gentle, willing to yield, full of mercy and good fruits, without partiality and without hypocrisy' (James 3:17). This is the kind of wisdom James had in mind."[3]

How may we avoid these errors? By loving the Lord Jesus Christ and thus His Word with all our hearts and desiring to please Him and bring glory to His Name. David internalized the Word of God because he had such a heart, as shown in his testimony thereunto, "O how I love your law; it is my meditation day and night" – Psalm 119-97. "How sweet are thy words unto my taste! yea, sweeter than honey to my mouth!"- Psalm 119-103. Jesus plainly said, "If you love me, you will obey my commandments" – John 14:15. The apostle John wrote, "The proof that you love is that you keep His commandments, and His commandments are not burdensome" – 1 John 5:3.

Thus the answer to Legalism, Ritualism, Meritorious Righteousness, and Partial Internalization is to obey our Lord Jesus Christ out of sheer love. If your motivation is anything else, you cannot succeed in internalizing the Word in a way that will bring glory to Jesus Christ and "joy and rejoicing" to your own soul – Jeremiah 15:16. The church at Ephesus performed many outward acts of righteousness, but having lost their "first love" for Jesus, they lost the reality of Jesus and He threatened to remove His light and mission from them – Revelation 2:1-4. Be a true "Internalizer of the Word," and you will discover "life and discover it more abundantly"- John 10:10b.

---

[3] Ibid. pp. 9-10.

Understanding Meditation

1. **Meditation** – Biblical meditation involves emptying the mind and filling it with God's Word. It is tuning out the world and tuning into a specific Scripture or attribute of God. Choose to block out everything else for a specific period of time. Focus upon Jesus and the words of the Bible.

   "This book of the law shall not depart from your mouth, but you shall meditate on it day and night, so that you may be careful to do according to all that is written in it; for then you will make your way prosperous, and then you will have 'good success' " – Joshua 1:8.

2. **Disconnection** – A time comes each day when we need to disconnect from the computer, the telephone, cell phones, pagers, VCRs, DVDs, TVs, and radios. In other words, disengaging from anything that beeps, blows, goes off, rings, honks, or says, "You've got mail." In sports it would be called a "time-out."

3. **Concentration** – "We need times of being still and simply listening to God. Too often we are moving targets, moving too quickly to hear what God has to say to us. Concentration is a way to practice silence before God. We deliberately think about God."[4]

"Blessed be the Lord who daily loads us with benefits." – Psalm 68:19

---

[4] Jay Dennis, *The Jesus Habits*, Nashville, Tennessee: B & H Publishing Group, 2005, p. 13.

30 Wonderful Benefits Of Internalizing The Word

1. ITW Keeps you in close relationship and intimacy with Jesus.
2. ITW Empowers you to overcome sinful lusts.
3. ITW Keeps your mind focused on Jesus.
4. ITW Enables you to take every thought captive to Christ.
5. ITW Deepens your understanding of God's Word dramatically.
6. ITW Increases your love for the living and written Word.
7. ITW Grows your faith dramatically.
8. ITW Enables you to answer accusations of Satan.
9. ITW Cleanses you of your sinful ways.
10. ITW Is a powerful deterrent to sin.
11. ITW Enables you to mediate on the Word day and night.
12. ITW Keeps you constantly refreshed and fruitful.
13. ITW Prevents you from backsliding.
14. ITW Makes your personal witness powerful, believable, and winning.
15. ITW Greatly strengthens your devotional life: worship and prayer.
16. ITW Makes your teaching and preaching authoritative, believable, and effective.
17. ITW Increases the confidence and response of your audience when speaking.
18. ITW Makes you an effective and courageous communicator.
19. ITW Equips you to be a Christian apologist (defender of the faith).
20. ITW Is a huge time saver.
21. ITW Assures you of excitement and vitality and joy.
22. ITW Cures boredom and prevents burnouts.
23. ITW Enables you to speak off the cuff.
24. ITW Makes you a constant discoverer of exciting truth.
25. ITW Qualifies you to be filled with the Holy Spirit.

26. ITW Assures you of real success and prosperity God's way.

27. ITW Enables you to be a Christ honoring conversationalist.

28. ITW Makes you especially useful in small group discussions.

29. ITW Enables you to mentor your family.

30. ITW Enables you to be a godly husband, father, Christian, church member, etc. having the character and conduct of Jesus or conforming into "Christ's image."

14 Simple Steps In Studying and Grasping The Bible

1. The Bible is one complete book. Those who skip the first 39 books will never understand the correct meaning of the rest. The Bible Jesus used was the 39 books of the Old Testament (Deut. 8:3; Luke 24:44ff) and also Paul and Timothy (2 Timothy 3:17-17).

2. You must know ALL the Scriptures on one subject to know what the Bible teaches. Example: Prayer – John 14:14 says you will get your prayers answered; but Isaiah 59:1-3 and James 4:2-3 says there are prayers God does not answer.

3. The Bible interprets the Bible. Example – The Book of Revelation is full of symbols, which are explained in Genesis, Daniel, etc, without which Revelation cannot be understood.

4. Be very careful to interpret every verse of Scripture according to its contextual setting. Example – Romans 10:13 says, "Whosoever shall call upon the Name of the Lord will be saved." Many take this verse to mean that all a person has to do to be saved is to get on his knees and ask the Lord to save him. But the verses following Romans 10:13 goes on to say that a person cannot call on One in whom he does not believe and he cannot believe on Him of whom he has not heard and to hear he must have a witness (Romans 10:14-15).

5. All the Bible is relevant and useful. "All Scripture is God-breathed and useful…" (2 Timothy 3:16). "Man shall not live by bread alone, but by every Word that proceeds out of the mouth of God." (Jesus, Matthew 4:4, quoting Deut. 8:3).

6. Do not expect to grasp the full meaning of all the Bible when you first study it. The great Bible expositor, Campbell Morgan wrote, "Often I do not understand what God is saying in a given Scripture. When I have this experience I am more convinced than ever that the Bible is God's Word, and the fact I don't understand it all confirms my conviction that it is the Word of God, not the Word of man. Then I bow my head and worship God."

7. The Word of God is inexhaustible in its treasures of truth and will continually reveal deeper truths as we meditate upon it and the Holy Spirit opens its true meaning. Example – Many times in my life I have carried a text in my heart and meditation for months and years before its full truth sprang forth to capture my heart and mind and give me the most powerful sermons I ever preached.

8. The Bible is open to the contrite and fearful heart (Psalm 25:14; Isaiah 66:2) and is closed to the prideful and self-sufficient. "...Jesus answered and said, "I thank you Father, Lord of heaven and earth, that you have hidden these things from the wise and prideful and revealed them to babes." (Matthew 11:25). Illus. Scholars from across the world assembled on the campus of Duke University to discuss the meaning of grace. While these intellectuals were wrangling over the subject, an uneducated, simple janitor in the hall was humming, "Amazing Grace, How Sweet the Sound..." A fellow student of mine passed by and said, "This simple man sweeping the floors knows more about grace than all these PhD's from around the world."

9. Pray without ceasing that God will reveal the truth of the Bible to your heart. (Psalm 25:4-5).

10. Prove the Bible by obeying it. God commands that we "prove all things" (1 Thess. 5:21). Illus. A noted scholar asked me this question one day, "Bill, how would you prove the existence of God?" I immediately replied, "Tithe." He laughed at me until I quoted Mal. 3:10 which invites the tither to tithe and he will see for himself how God will keep His promise to bless those who do.

11. You can prove almost anything from the Bible, but only if you interpret verses out of context. Example – Recently I heard a widely known TV evangelist teach that God promises His people 120 years, not 70. In fact he boasted that he would live 120 years himself. He did so by taking Genesis 6:3 out of context. In this verse the Lord

warned that His Spirit would not strive with man forever, but that there would be a delay of 120 years before the judgment of the flood would occur.

12. The Bible sheds a lot of light on the commentaries. Great errors have been passed down through generations because some commentator was believed rather than the Bible. Example – the famous Scofield Bible divides Christians into two classes:

   a. Spiritual, and

   b. Carnal, but the Apostle Paul makes it crystal clear that the "carnal mind is enmity against God and is not subject to the law of God, nor indeed can be" (Romans 8:7) and that Christians are "not in the flesh (not carnal) but in the Spirit...(Romans 9:9). Yet, vast numbers of evangelicals, following Scofield's Bible, teach and preach the two kinds of believers, leaving multitudes in my opinion in their sins and lost who believe they are saved.

13. No translation of the Bible is perfect. I love the language of the original or the New King James version and have memorized from them, but there are deficiencies in them- Transliterated words:

   a. "Baptize" which if translated would have read "immersed" and would have avoided much confusion through the centuries.

   b. "Deacon" which means servant, not a church boss. Many deacons think the term "deacon" is an honorary title which bestows upon them the right to run the church and dictate to the pastor. This false impression has resulted in serious troubles in many local churches through the years.

   c. Acts 19:2 – The word "after" should be "when." "After" leaves the impression that you receive the Holy Spirit after you're saved when in reality you receive the Holy Spirit the moment you're saved (Romans 8:9b).

14. The best translation of the Bible is "The gospel according to Tom, Dick and Harry." Dr. Donald Barnhouse said the world may never read the Bible in leather or morocco, but it will never fail to read the Bible in shoe leather." What do people see when they read the gospel according to your life?

Chapter 2

Infilling of the Holy Spirit

The ministry of the Holy Spirit is absolutely indispensable in the life of any person who would be "conformed to the image of Christ" and serve Him effectively; for it is the work of the Holy Spirit to make real in our lives what Christ has provided for us in His death, burial and resurrection. God the Father *thought* our salvation; God the Son *bought* our salvation, and the Holy Spirit *brought* us salvation (Ephesians 1:3-13).

When I began to preach I knew the Holy Spirit was of utmost importance in the Christian life, but I knew very little of how He works in human experience. But I was hungry to know, and He taught me seven monumental truths:

1. The Holy Spirit is a Person.

2. He comes into our lives when we repent, trust Christ, and are born again.

3. He baptizes us into the body of Christ simultaneously with our new birth.

4. He indwells us and our bodies become His temple.

5. He fills and refills with the Holy Spirit which is followed by His anointing.

6. He never glorifies Himself but Jesus only.

7. He reproduces in us the blessings Jesus has provided for us in His death, burial, and resurrection.

The *new birth* and consequent indwelling represent our salvation; the *baptism* represents our spiritual position in Christ, the *infilling* represents our spiritual condition, and the *anointing* represents our vocation, that is, our empowerment to exercise our spiritual gifts – the "special touch for the special task." To be anointed one must:

(1) Live a life of holiness,

(2) Live a life of yieldedness, and

(3) Live a life of prayerfulness. [5]

I was saved at the age of nine. Thus I was born of the Holy Spirit, indwelt by His presence, baptized into the body of Christ, but not filled until I was 34 years old. It happened on the streets of Greensboro and at a time of desperate need. My experience was not an emotional one. I saw no angels. I did not go into a trance. I did not speak in tongues. I did not swoon, nor was I "slain in the Spirit." I was overwhelmingly conscious in my spirit that the Holy Spirit was with me and beside me and walking with me. I saw no physical person. But I was as conscious of the presence of the Holy Spirit as I would have been if my wife in her physical body had been walking beside me. In a word, the Holy Spirit revealed Himself to me in the way Jesus had promised He would: The PARAKLETOS (John 14:16), ONE like Himself Who would be called beside His children forever. I cannot describe the assurance that came over my soul. I knew without a doubt that I was not alone in living a godly life and experiencing a powerful ministry, but that I dared not speak of it publicly for a long time and now only cautiously and reverently. However, one can't hide anything from his wife though he tries. Thus within an hour or less when I joined my wife, she turned to me and asked, "Bill, what has happened to you?" I replied, "Has something happened that is unusual?" She replied, "Yes." Then I asked, "Is it something good or bad?" She replied, "Good." At that point I shared of my encounter with the Holy Spirit on Davie Street in downtown Greensboro. Since then I have heard my wife say time and time again, "I received a new husband that day and our marriage became a joy." As for myself I do not mean to imply that my encounter with the Holy Spirit that day exempted me from some struggles, disappointments, hardships, even some "Dark Gethsemane" nights. But I do say that though I have found myself at times in the valley, I have never doubted that the wonderful *Parakletos* was with me and would sustain me in the darkest hour. In those moments I have experienced many "infillings." My encounter occurred some fifty years ago, however, and I continue to draw immeasurable strength from it. At the present, I sense in my life His overflowing love, joy, hope and power

---

[5] Stephen Olford

as I pour my life into hundreds of men who seek to become true Christ followers.

Collateral Material On The Second "I"

Understanding The Indispensable Role Of The Holy Spirit In The Christian Life.

If one would know Jesus Christ and keep growing in His grace, he must understand and appropriate the work of the Holy Spirit in his life.

A Mini Course on the Person and Work of the Holy Spirit:

1. *Attitudes* Toward the Holy Spirit:
   a. Ignorance – Acts 19:2
   b. Indifference
   c. Ignition
2. *Attributes* of the Holy Spirit:
   a. Person
   b. God
   c. Jesus' Personal Representative in the world today
3. *Advantages* of the Coming of the Holy Spirit – John 16:7-11 (See page 22)
4. *Accomplishments* of the Holy Spirit:
   a. The Virgin Birth – Matthew 1:20; Luke 1:35
   b. The New Birth – the key to his baptism, indwelling, infilling, and out-going.
5. *Acceptance:*
   a. Repent and trust Jesus as Lord and Savior – Acts 2:38

D. L. Moody, "You can eat without a tongue, breath without lungs, see without eyes, sooner than you can live the Christian life without the Holy Spirit."

When Jesus announced to His disciples that He would soon be departing from them, great sorrow filled their hearts, for they assumed they would be left in this world without a Teacher, Guide, Power, or Comforter (John 16:1-5). But Jesus assured His followers that they would be better off after His departure than they were with His presence (John 6:7-11). How could this possibly be? Jesus sets forth the specific advantages that would occur:

1. **Jesus would prepare a place in heaven for His followers after His departure.** "I go to prepare a place for you" (John 14:2). Many have thought Jesus went to heaven to build the place called heaven, using His great carpentry skills. Primarily what Jesus meant was that He was going to Calvary (the Cross) to die for sinners that they might be forgiven and saved and made ready for the home in heaven. As the hymn says, "The Way of the Cross Leads Home," and Jesus had to die before that home was ready.

2. **The Holy Spirit has come to be our Great Comforter by coming "alongside" of us under all circumstances.** Jesus said "And I will pray to the Father that He send you another Comforter that He may abide with you forever" (John 14:16). The Greek word translated Comforter is *Parakletos* which means "called alongside to assist." True comfort strengthens us to face life bravely and keep on going. The Holy Spirit does not rob us of our responsibility but enables us to stay in the race and not give up. Some translators call the Holy Spirit "the Encourager," and I would call Him the "Great Encourager." Also the "Great Remembrancer" (John 14:26).

3. **The disciples would experience Jesus in a more personal way after the coming of the Holy Spirit than they did before.** "I will not leave you spiritual orphans: I am coming to you" (John 14:18). What Jesus meant was "My departure will not be like that of a Father whose children are left orphans when he dies. In the Spirit I am coming back to you." The Holy Spirit reveals Jesus, glorifies Him, applies His blood and merits to the hearts of believers, makes His teachings effective in their lives. Hence, when the Spirit was poured out, Christ truly returned. Liberals, desiring to deny the Second Coming, have said the coming of the Holy Spirit is the Second Coming, but not true.

4. **The disciples would be enabled to "do greater works" than they had ever witnessed Jesus Himself doing in the days of His flesh.** "Verily, verily, I say unto you, He that believeth on me, the works that I do shall he do also; and greater works than these shall he do; because I go unto my Father" (John 14:12). This would be possible, for after the coming of the Holy Spirit at Pentecost every believer would have the presence and power of Jesus in them through the Person of the Holy Spirit. Prior to the coming of the Holy Spirit, Jesus was limited to one locale at a given time. After Pentecost He is present in every believer and every believer is to witness of His saving grace, resulting in multitudes being saved (Acts 2:41).

5. **Jesus went to heaven and sent the Holy Spirit to live in the heart of all believers, so that they might be powerful witnesses of His saving grace.** "When the Spirit is come (to the church) He (the Holy Spirit) will convict the world of *Sin,* of *Righteousness,* and of *Judgment.* Of sin, because they believe not on me; of righteousness, because I go to my Father and you will see me no more, of judgment because the prince of this world (Satan) is judged" (John 16:8-11). "But you shall receive power when the Holy Spirit has come upon you; and you shall be witnesses to Me both in Jerusalem, and in all Judea and Samaria, and to the end of the earth" (Acts 1:8).

It is important that we note that the Holy Spirit comes to believers (the church) and not to the world. This means He works in and through you and me if we are born again. The Holy Spirit does not minister in a vacuum. Just as Jesus had a body in order to do His work on earth, so the Holy Spirit needs a body to accomplish His ministries and that body is His redeemed church. Our bodies are His temples and tools, and He wants to use us for His glory. Illus: Often we hear people pray, "Lord, send your Holy Spirit to speak to the lost." Such praying sounds good, but is it biblical? Many think the Holy Spirit "floats" up and down the pews in a ghostly manner. No, the Holy Spirit works through His people in whom He lives. This does not mean the Sovereign Holy Spirit could never speak directly to someone, but it does mean that He speaks primarily through believers who are surrendered to Him. I sense very little of the Holy Spirit's convictions in churches today. This means one tragic thing: Members of the church are not instruments through which the Holy Spirit can convict the lost because they are grieving (Ephesians 4:30 and quenching (1 Thess. 5;19) the Holy Spirit.

What does the Holy Spirit do through believers? Jesus said "He convicts or reproves the world of three things" (John 16:8). The word "convict" means "to convict and convince," or simply to pronounce the verdict. Believers are the witnesses, the Holy Spirit is the prosecuting attorney, and the unsaved are the guilty prisoners:

1. **The Holy Spirit convicts the world of one particular sin: The Sin of Unbelief.** The conscience will convict men of their sins, but only the Holy Spirit can convict the lost of unbelief. After all, it is unbelief that condemns the sinner and sends him to hell (John 3:18-21), not the committing of individual sins. A person could "clean up his life" and quit his bad habits and still be lost and go to hell. Many seek to win the lost by seeking to persuade them to quit drinking, etc., never showing them that their damning sin is the rejection of Jesus as Savior and Lord.

2. **The Holy Spirit convicts the world of Righteousness, not unrighteousness.** Whose righteousness? The Righteousness of Jesus, who returned and was received by His Father in heaven to show He was righteous. Men must see their righteousnesses as "filthy rags" (Isaiah 64:6) and know that the only righteousness that will save is that of Jesus Himself.

3. **The Holy Spirit convicts the world of judgment.** "Of judgment because the prince of this world (Satan) is judged." Jesus is saying that just as Satan has already been judged and sentenced, so will the sinner who persist in unbelief and rejection of the true righteousness of Jesus.

In a word, there can be no true conversion without conviction of sin, righteousness, and judgment, and there can be no conversion apart from the Spirit of God using the Word of God generally through the witness of the child of God. Do you not see how Christians desperately need to understand and surrender to the Holy Spirit? Yet the fact is that most believers believe only that they need to accept Jesus as their Savior and are either totally ignorant or indifferent to the wonderful work of the Holy Spirit. But as D. L. Moody said, "You can eat without a tongue, breath without lungs, see without eyes, sooner than you can live the Christian life without the Holy Spirit."

Illus.: As a young pastor I knew from reading the New Testament that the Holy Spirit was crucial in the Christian life, so I approached an "elder" statesman expressing my concern that we honor the Holy Spirit, and he replied, "Bill, don't bother with the Holy Spirit; just preach Jesus," not realizing that we experience the life of Jesus only through the Holy Spirit.

Illus.: When I was discouraged, tired, defeated, depressed, and ready to give up, the Holy Spirit joined me on the streets of Greensboro, assuring me of His glorious presence and helper for every need I had. That was the beginning of a new day in my personal life, my marriage, and my ministry.

The Holy Spirit Passionately Yearns For You – James 4:5

One of the most amazing truths concerning the love of the Holy Spirit for every single child of God is hid away in the little book of James, chapter four, verse 5. "Do ye think that the Scripture saith in vain, The spirit that dwelleth in us lusteth to envy?" The key word in the verse is *Lust*, which is the Greek word, *epipotheo*, meaning an intense desire, a craving, hunger, a yearning, longing or pining for something. What does the Holy Spirit yearn for so passionately that the Bible would picture Him that way? He yearns that each believer give his time, devotion and total surrender to Him so that He may produce the life of Christ in Him. That should not surprise us. He is our life through the new birth, our Indweller, our Controller (filler), Sealer, Sanctifier, and Source of power. The word *epipotheo* (lust) means that the Holy Spirit wants all of us, or as one commentator observed, "The Holy Spirit can never get enough of us." In Romans 12:1 God through the Apostle Paul is begging us to "present our bodies as a living sacrifice." This verse does not say to whom we should present our bodies. However, we know it is not to God the Father who is heaven and needs no body; it is not God the Son, for He already has a body. So that leaves it to be the "Holy Spirit," who has no body, except the bodies of born again individuals. Just think – you are the dwelling place, the residence, the home of the living God through the Holy Spirit. Thus the Holy Spirit is jealous to claim all of you for the glory of Christ, for whom He has come to glorify. Will you permit Him to do so NOW?

I. Understanding the Work of the Father, the Son and the Holy Spirit in Redemption

The Father, Son and Holy Spirit are active in every step of redemption. However, there is a difference in the function of each. It is necessary to recognize the differences in operation in order to cooperate in the fulfillment of God's purpose for our lives.

To make the difference simple, we could say that the Father *prescribes* redemption, the Son *provides* redemption, and the Holy Spirit *applies* redemption. Or the Father *thought* redemption, the Son *bought* redemption, and the Holy Spirit *brought* redemption. Or as one theologian put it, "God is the originating cause; God the Son is the mediating cause, and God the Holy Spirit is the effecting cause (Dr. James McKee Adams). These three roles are set forth in chapter one of Ephesians.

A practical illustration of the teamwork of the Trinity in redemption:

A striking analogy is afforded in the realm of medicine. "There are three professions involved in the treatment of disease: the physician who diagnoses the case and prescribes the treatment; the pharmacist who compounds the remedy; and the nurse who faithfully waits at the patient's bedside and administers that which the doctor has prescribed and the druggist prepared. In the analogy, of course, the physician represents the Father, who has diagnosed the need of the sinner and prescribed the remedy. The druggist represents the Son, who by achieving a perfect human life, provides through His shed blood the only specific cure of sin. The nurse represents the Holy Spirit, who applies the remedy by quickening the Word to challenge the faith of the sinner.[6]

I love this analogy because it pictures the loving and practical nature of the part of the Holy Spirit in recovery from the disease of sin. Anyone who has ever been seriously sick knows what it means to have a compassionate and loving nurse at his or her bedside, administering every aid and literally pulling him through his illness. Such is the wonderful ministry of the Holy Spirit.

---

[6] Ralph Herring, God Being My Helper, Nashville, Tennessee: Broadman Press, 1955, pp. 10-11.

II. The Crucifixion of King Self

The greatest problem by far, that anyone of us faces, is the problem of Self. King Self is the chief hindrance to being filled with the Holy Spirit. What is Self? It is the rebellious, even incorrigible, nature of every human, passed down from Adam, which seeks its own way, pleasure, comfort, viewpoint, etc. with little or no regard for the rights of others. Paul's word for this attitude is flesh.

The big question is, how we can gain victory over this ungodly disposition? To make this victory ours is the first work of the Holy Spirit after that of regeneration (the new birth). The way the Holy Spirit gives this victory is by the "crucifixion (or death) of the flesh" (Romans 8:13).

Now positionally , every true believer is already dead to sin through the cross (including self) and alive to God through the resurrection (Romans 6:4). In accepting Christ, he accepts Christ's death to sin (Gal. 2:20). Having been crucified with Him, it is only natural that he would be buried with Him also, for after death comes burial. Hence in God's sight the rebel self, the big "I" is dead and buried. However, the young believer does not journey far before he discovers through painful experience that if self is dead, it is the livest dead thing he has ever encountered. Paul testifies to this dilemma and cries out "O wretched man I am. Who shall deliver me from the body of death?" (Roman. 7:24).

The question is: how can the flesh be put to death in our experience?

1. Certainly not by the energy of the flesh. Some pray, "Lord, help me crucify myself?" Multitudes rededicate their lives, seeking to overcome the flesh, but such is only the rededication of the flesh.

2. The flesh must be crucified. But how? No man can crucify himself. It is a physical impossibility. One may commit suicide in many different ways, but if he ever dies by crucifixion, someone else will put him on the cross.

3. The Holy Spirit is God's agent to bring crucifixion to pass. As Romans 8:13 specifically states, "If you by the Spirit do put to death the deeds of the body, you shall life." However, to understand how the Spirit works with us to put the death sentence into effect, we must understand the words, "put to death." These three words are one word in Greek, *thanatoute,* which literally means "to cause to be

put to death" the "deeds of the body." Note: the "deeds of the body," (or doing's of the body) meaning acts of evil which come through the body, not the body itself.

4. We cannot crucify ourselves. We are only to give the Holy Spirit the permission to get it done. We must say the word, because God does nothing in us without our own active cooperation.

Illustration of Crucifixion: The best way I know to explain crucifixion is to quote the words of a brother who impacted my life as no other person I ever knew in understanding the mysterious work of the Holy Spirit. So here goes:

"An experience some years ago brought home to me this aspect of the Holy Spirit's ministry. We had at that time a pet dog named Skipper which had won his way into our affections – especially those of our children. One day Skipper was struck by a passing automobile. Though he recovered in a measure from his injury, Skipper was never himself again. His disposition was ruined and he became a problem in the neighborhood. One day after he had snapped at my little daughter I sent him to the veterinarian for observation. The doctor explained that sometimes a dog's disposition was permanently altered by an injury of that nature. He stated that Skipper would probably be a dangerous pet to have with the little children in the home and frankly advised me to put him out of the way.

The veterinarian had made his recommendation. He stood ready to carry out the course that he had advised. But the problem was mine – the dog was mine, and the children were mine. It was my responsibility to say the word, and I said it. I have always felt that I said the right word, and ever since I have held in grateful appreciation the friend who counseled me so wisely and who then so faithfully did the "dirty work" for me. So far as I know that is the only sentence of execution I have pronounced – except that which time and time again I pronounce when the Holy Spirit reveals to me the working of a vicious nature within and waits my word to carry out the death sentence which he so strongly recommends.

My relation to Skipper in the incident referred to above designates the position which the believer must take in regard to the problem of self. But the act of pronouncing God's sentence must be cultivated until it becomes a habit of mind. That attitude is described in Romans 6:11 where Paul say, "Even so reckon ye also yourselves to be dead unto sin, but alive unto God in Christ Jesus." The tense of the verb is present, indicating a continuing process of reckoning. The figure is that of a bookkeeper making his entries, or of a navigator setting his course in a given direction. Appearances to the contrary, our old man has been crucified, as God's Word plainly states. "Ye died, and your life is hid with Christ in God" (Col. 3:3). "They that are of Christ Jesus have crucified the flesh with the passions and the lusts thereof" (Gal. 5:24). The inference is unavoidable. The thing is done. The crucifixion has already taken place. By faith we must accept the bearings God has given us and hold to the course in a steady reckoning."[7]

A final caution: This business of being "dead to sin" (crucified) does not necessarily take away its appeal, nor does it render us incapable of responding. We are free to do as we choose. But God's perfect will is that we "play" by His rules, and the Holy Spirit is yearning for us to do so (James 4:5). His rule is this: Quietly reckon ourselves to be dead unto sin and alive unto God as He has said (Romans 6:11). And the wonderful thing is that when we make His reckoning a "lifestyle" and take the position that we are dead to sin (including self) and do not have to commit it and are alive to God, the victory is ours, as we find ourselves being filled moment by moment by the Holy Spirit and walking in His power.

What's The Big Deal About Fruit?

Jesus said, "By their fruits you shall know them" (Matthew 5:20).

1. **Your fruit reveals your identity.** Illus.: In nature you know a tree is a peach tree if it bears peaches. In the kingdom you know a person possesses the Holy Spirit, if he bears the fruit of the Holy Spirit (Gal. 5:22). If not, you know he does not have the Holy Spirit.

2. **Your fruit reveals your spiritual health.** True naturally, also true spiritually. Illus.: I noted recently a very sick tree in my back yard. How did I know it was sick? It had no life nor leaves. Illus.: I observe people all the time, some of them at close sight. On some I find great fruit; others I find no fruit. If a natural tree has no fruit, you know it is

---

[7] Ibid. pp. 25-25.

dead; if a professing Christian has no fruit, you can know He is dead (James 2:26).

3. **Your fruit reveals God's purpose for your life, which should also be your purpose. A natural tree does not produce fruit for itself but for others. Likewise, the spiritual fruit is for others to eat and nourish their souls.** Illus.: The Spirit-filled life is described as a flowing river going out of one's innermost being into the lives of others. "He who believes on me as the Scriptures say, out of his inner being shall flow rivers of living waters" (John 7:37). I believe there are nine of these rivers flowing from any Spirit-filled person (Gal. 5:22-23):

   a. A river of love

   b. Joy

   c. Peace

   d. Patience

   e. Gentleness (kindness)

   f. Goodness

   g. Faithfulness

   h. Meekness

   i. Self-control

Thus the ultimate purpose of the Spirit-filled life is not primarily to make us happy, or emotional or flashy, but to make us winning witnesses for Jesus Christ, soul-winners if you like. "When the Holy Spirit is come upon you, you shall receive power and you shall be witnesses unto me in Jerusalem, Judea, Samaria, and to the uttermost parts of the earth." (Acts 1:8).

The fruit of a Spirit-filled Christian is another Christian. Only 5 percent of professing believers ever witness and of those who witness, very, very, very few bring the lost to a saving knowledge and confession of Jesus Christ as Lord and Savior. What does this tell us about the need for God's people to be Spirit-filled?

Illus.: A faithful member of our Mentoring School mailed me the following powerful illustration, showing how we can be continually filled with the Holy Spirit.

26

An illustration of being filled by the Holy Spirit by Rick Simpson

"Picture a powerful rushing river, this living water represents the Holy Spirit. Picture us as empty vessels, a cylinder open on both ends like a paper towel roll. We are submersed, baptized, engulfed by the living water. We are completely filled from top to bottom and the river's current rushes past us. The empty vessel, now totally filled, becomes stagnant until the cylinder, our life, is turned sideways in the direction the river is flowing. Still totally filled, same water, but now it rushes thru the vessel with the power of the river, unrestricted, freely flowing through and being constantly renewed simply by changing the orientation of the cylinder.

When my mind wrapped around this picture it helped me with the questions; Am I not filled up all the way? Am I saved, then "zapped" by the Holy Spirit later? How can I be filled and have no power? Is the Holy Spirit leaking out of my vessel & what happens when I'm empty? The Scripture says be continually filled but I thought I was filled?

The answer: I'm filled with the Holy Spirit but my life is somewhere between 0 & 90 degrees. Standing straight up I'm filled and on my own but when I offer to lay down my life in alignment with the direction of the Holy Spirit – power flows through me. Not for me, not because of me and not even controlled by me…it just does."

Understanding The Infilling Of The Holy Spirit – Ephesians 5:17-18

Next to the new birth there is nothing more important for a Christian to understand and to experience than that of the infilling of the Holy Spirit. In order to understand this glorious truth, we must raise and answer some crucial questions.

I. **What Is The New Birth of The Holy Spirit?** The new birth of the Holy Spirit is the entrance of the Holy Spirit into our lives when we truly repent of our sins and surrender our lives to Jesus. When this occurs the Holy Spirit regenerates us or gives us a new birth. This marks one's entrance into the kingdom of God and assures one of his salvation (John 3:3,5).

II. **What Is The Baptism of The Holy Spirit?** The baptism of the Holy Spirit is the gracious act by which the Holy Spirit baptizes or incorporates each believer into the body of the living Christ (1 Cor. 12:13). This baptism is a once-for-all unrepeatable act of God. The baptism occurs at the time of the new birth. Thus the Bible never commands us to be baptized by the Holy Spirit, since that act occurred the moment one trusts Jesus as Lord and Savior.

III. **What Is The Indwelling of The Holy Spirit?** The indwelling is the presence of the Holy Spirit (the same as the Spirit of Christ) which begins the moment one is born again of the Holy Spirit and will continue until the day of redemption (resurrection of the body) (Ephesians 4:30). The Holy Spirit indwells the body of every believer, making our bodies the "temples of the Holy Spirit" (1 Cor. 6:19-0). This permanent indwelling began on the Day of Pentecost when the Holy Spirit transferred His place of abode from the throne in heaven into the bodies of all believers, and "if any person has not the Spirit of Christ, he does not belong to Christ" (Romans 8:9b; Acts 19:2).

IV. **What Is The Sealing of The Holy Spirit?** This means that every true believer receives the Spirit of God as a sign that he belongs to God and that he will be kept safe by God until the time he receives his glorified body. Just as in legal matters, a seal indicates ownership and security, so it does in divine affairs. The indwelling brands us as God's property (1 Cor. 6:19-20) and guarantees our preservation until the day of redemption (Ephesians 4:30).

V. **What Is The Infilling of The Holy Spirit?** The infilling of the Holy Spirit is the control of the Holy Spirit over the believer's life and occurs when one surrenders his life completely to the control of the Holy Spirit. Luke 5:26 states that the disciples were "filled" with fear, meaning they were controlled or dominated by the emotion of fear. The word "filled" in Luke 5:26 is the same word found in Ephesians 5:18, "Be ye filled with the Holy Spirit." While the baptism of the Holy Spirit occurs only once, the infilling may occur at a crisis moment, but it continually occurs as one surrenders to the Holy Spirit. Examples: Stephen Olford, Billy Graham, and myself.

VI. **What Are The Great Hindrances To Being Filled And Continually Filled?**

1. The grieving of the Holy Spirit (Ephesians 4:30).

2. The quenching of the Holy Spirit (1 Thess. 5:19).

3. Ignorance of the truth and necessity for the infilling (Ephesians 5:17).

VII. **Can One Lose The Infilling?** Indeed he can and often does.

VIII. **Why Do We Need To Be Filled When We Already Have The Holy Spirit Through The New Birth?** Through the new birth, the Holy Spirit indwells us. He is present and resident within us. But He can be present and resident without being president. Unfortunately when the Holy Spirit comes to live within us, we often push Him off into a closet or some dark wing of our soul. Then He has no access to the TV room, the master bedroom, the kitchen, the refrigerator, etc. – that is, He is resident but He isn't president.

IX. **What Is The Relationship Of The Average Church Member To The Holy Spirit?** It is my experience that the average church is filled with three different kinds of people:

1. Those who come to church but don't know the Lord at all. The Holy Spirit doesn't live within them, so they can't be filled with Him.

2. Those who come to church who are Christians and the Holy Spirit lives within them, but they never give Him control of their lives.

3. Those who have consciously and knowingly given over their lives to the Spirit's control.

X. **Why Do We Need To Be Filled With The Holy Spirit?**

1. You must be filled to be obedient to God's commands (Ephesians 5:18).

2. You must be filled to fulfill the requirements of the Christian life. Example: "Jesus commands,...Thou shalt love the Lord thy God with all thy heart, and with all thy soul, and with all thy mind. This is the first and great commandment. And the second is like unto it, Thou shalt love thy neighbour as thyself. (Matthew 22:37-39). How can I attain that?

   Scripture says, 'Rejoice always, pray without ceasing, in everything give thanks' (1 Thessalonians 5:16-18). Who can live like that?

   Scripture says, 'Take captive every thought to make it obedient to Christ.' (2 Cor. 10:5, NIV). Every thought? How in the world could I do that?

   Scripture says, 'Do good to those who hate you, and pray for those who spitefully use you and persecute you' (Matthew 5:44). Even on the freeway, Lord?

   These standards, and many more I could mention, are just...well, impossible. If we don't have a power that is beyond us as human beings, we can't live the Christian life."[8]

3. You must be filled in order to exercise your spiritual gifts (1 Cor. 12:7).

4. You must be filled to receive the anointing (1 Cor. 1:21).

5. You must be filled to walk in victory (Romans 15:13).

6. You must be filled to overcome the flesh (Romans 8:13).

XI. Who Is Commanded To Be Filled? Ephesians 5:18 answers this question.

1. This command is in the *imperative* mood. It isn't optional. Every believer is commanded to be filled and controlled by the Spirit.

2. The command is *plural* which means that the command is given to all of us – not just to "super saints" or "spiritual giants."

3. The command is in the passive voice. This means we don't fill ourselves. The filling comes from an outside source – the Holy Spirit.

---

[8] David Jeremiah, *God in You*, Sisters, Oregon: Multonomah Publishers, 1998, pp. 76-77.

4. The command is in the present tense. This means the filling is a repeated event.

XII. **What Are The Requirements To Be Filled?** Assuming you already have the Holy Spirit through the new birth, you must meet the following conditions.

1. **Desire to be filled.** Being filled begins with desire. As a good football coach tells his embattled troops at half-time, "Guys, you gotta want to." Jesus said "If anyone thirst or hunger, he shall be filled." (Matthew 5:6; John 7:37). Does this describe you? Are you thirsty – maybe a little desperate – for a closer walk with God? Do you ever find yourself crying out with the psalmist, 'My soul thirsts for God, for the living God. When shall I come and appear before God?' (Psalm 42:2).

   Jesus said that when the Holy Spirit controls you, you will have a hunger and a thirst to know God and grow in Him. Out of this acute, life-defining thirst comes the Spirit-controlled life."[9]

2. **Denounce all the known sin in your life.** "Confession of sin is critical, but denunciation is a step beyond confession. I might confess to a problem with impure thoughts, but what good does that do if I go out and buy a Playboy magazine this afternoon? Paul explained it like this:

   'Since we have these promises, dear friends, let us purify ourselves from everything that contaminates the body and spirit, perfecting holiness out of reverence for God' (2 Cor. 7:1, NIV).

   When we come to be filled with the Spirit, we have to cleanse our hearts through the shed blood of the Lord Jesus Christ. We have to say, 'God, if there is any sin in my life, if there's something I'm doing that isn't pleasing to You, put Your finger on it. Show me what it is, and Lord, I will denounce it. I will confess it, and I will turn from it.

   You can't be filled with the Holy Spirit while you're harboring your own little pet sins. Maybe it's a place to which you go, a relationship in which you're involved, the types of entertainment you indulge

---

[9] Ibid, Jeremiah, p. 81.

31

in, or a habit you've clung to for years—something that you know violates God's standards. You will never be filled with the Spirit of God until you denounce it, confess it, and forsake it. The Holy Spirit isn't just a title, that's who He is, and He doesn't enjoy living in an unclean environment. If there is known, unconfessed sin in your life, the Holy Spirit will not take control. The very fact of your sin is evidence that He isn't in control."[10]

3. **Die to self** (2 Cor. 4:10). To be filled with the Spirit is to yield to His control. It is to take self off the throne of your heart and enthrone Jesus. Romans 12:1-2 are absolute keys to the Spirit-controlled life.

4. **Depend fully upon the Holy Spirit.** A better word is surrender. Surrender is just the opposite of rededication of life or what we call commitment. When we commit to the Lord, we name the terms of our commitment. When we surrender, we let Him set the terms. Illus.: Just suppose Jesus was standing before you and asked you to demonstrate your commitment on a blank sheet of paper He would hand to you. He would not ask you to list on the paper the things you would commit and then sign your name at the bottom. He would just ask you to sign your name at the bottom, and He would fill in over your signature what He would expect and require.

In summary, the requirements are:

(1) I want to be filled – *desire*

(2) I want to get rid of the sin in my life – *denounce*

(3) I want to give control of myself to God – *die*

(4) I am depending absolutely on the Holy Spirit – *dependence* or surrender.

XIII.   What Are The Consequences Of Being Filled?

1. When you are filled you reflect the character of Jesus (Galatians 5:22-23).

2. When you are filled, you have victory over indwelling sin (Galatians 5:16).

3. When you are filled, the Bible comes alive (1 Cor. 2:14).

---

[10] Ibid., Jeremiah, pp. 81-82

4. When you are filled, prayer is urgent and compelling (Romans 8:26).

5. When you are filled, you have constant fellowship with the living Christ (John 14:21).

6. When you are filled, you have boldness to witness (Acts 1:8; Acts 4:31).

7. When you are filled, you have great joy (Acts 13:51).

8. When you are filled you are empowered to keep the moral law of God (Romans 8:2-4).

9. When filled, Jesus lives his life through you. Paul testifies to this experience in Gal. 2:20. Illus.: Only if Christ is living in you can you live the Christian life. Suppose I went to play basketball and tried to take the place of Michael Jordan. Could I? Absolutely not. But suppose I showed up and played as well or better than Jordan. How could that be? If Michael Jordan took up his residence within, then he could play the game for me. So it is with the infilling. (Gal. 2:20).

The one indisputable proof of being filled with the Holy Spirit – the fruit of the Holy Spirit

The beautiful fruit of the Holy Spirit is understood best when viewed in the light of the ugly works of the flesh. Thus in the Bible, Paul first identifies the "works of the flesh" (Galatians 5:19-21) and then follows with the "fruit of the Holy Spirit."

1. **The flesh produces works.** The word "work" in Greek is *Ergos*, meaning hard work or labor. A life dominated by the flesh, which is the life style of any unsaved person, is filled with bitterness, excesses, imbalance, self-abuse, laziness, strife, irresponsibility, depression, emptiness, and finally death. It is the hardest route for any individual to take. Yet the flesh cries out to be in charge, screaming to have its own way, demanding to be the boss, all the time promising to bring happiness and fulfillment, when in reality it brings emptiness, frustration, horror, and death – in a word ungodliness. Illus: Like drinking salt water, the more you drink, the thirstier you become.

2. **The Holy Spirit produces fruit,** and the life filled with the Holy Spirit brings forth godliness, the very character of Jesus (God) into

our hearts and actions. What produces the fruit? All fruit is produced by some kind of seed. The moment you were born again God sowed His Spirit and Word into your heart like a seed, and you were made spiritually alive by "the incorruptible seed of the Word of God" (1 Peter 1:23). Just like apples produce apples, oranges produce oranges, God's seed in you immediately begins to produce God-like fruits.

Paul lists nine expressions of the "fruit of the Holy Spirit" in Galatians 5:22-23. The great expositor, G. Campbell Morgan, believed that all 8 pieces of the fruit of the Spirit is contained in the authentic love of God (agape). So Galatians 5:22-23 could well be translated like this, "The fruit of the Spirit is love, that is, joy, love, peace, long suffering, gentleness, goodness, faith, meekness and temperance." The Apostle John seems to imply the same truth in 1 John 4:7-8, "Love is of God and everyone who loves is born of God and knowth God." And Paul writes, "The love of God is poured out in our hearts by the Holy Spirit which is given unto us." (Romans 5:5).

Since love capsulates all the fruit of the Holy Spirit, we must ask, "What kind of love?" There are four primary Greek words to describe the various expressions of love:

1. **Eros love** – a term for sexual love, where we get the word erotic. It is significant that this word never appears in the New Testament, not even in the context of sex in marriage.

2. **Stergo love** – the love that exists between parents and children.

3. **Phileo love** – the love between two persons who feel compatible and well matched.

4. **Agape love** – a love that has no strings attached, divine love not looking for what it can get from another but what it can give to that person for his very highest welfare, spiritually, physically, emotionally, psychologically.

Thus you can see the limitations of human love compared to Agape:

1. **Eros** – is self-seeking

2. **Stergo** – is limited only to your family

3. **Phileo** – is based on mutual satisfaction

4. **Agape** – is totally unselfish, not limited to one's family, not dependant on mutual benefits, but totally self-giving, absolutely sacrificial, never conditioned by circumstances. The best example of Agape love is found in the best known verse in the entire Bible, John 3:16, "For God so loved (Agapao) the world…"

Now let us observe how Agape sharply contrast with the other expressions of love and what Agape love looks like in the common relationships of life:

1. If Eros is the basis of your sexual relationship with your spouse instead Agape, you will be self-centered and focused only on your needs, which does not long satisfy and accounts for many divorces. But if your relationship is based on Agape, you will seek to serve and please your spouse and your marriage will improve rather than deteriorate.

2. If Phileo is the basis of your friendship, you will be a "come and go" friend and faithful only as long as you get what you want out of the relationship. If Agape is the basis, you will be a faithful, immovable friend for life.

3. If Stergo is the basis of your love for your family, you will live in disappointments all your life, but if based on Agape, you will always be devoted to your family no matter the disappointments.

4. If Agape is the driving motivation of your life and the force behind all your relationships, you will be the best, reliable, faithful, helpful, understanding individual anyone has ever known. In a word you will be conformed to the image of Christ. To put it another way:

a. Your relationship with God will be marked by love, joy and peace

b. Your relationship with *others* will be marked by longsuffering (patience), gentleness (kindness), goodness

c. Your relationship with *yourself* will be marked by meekness, self-control and faithfulness.

"Love in a Word is the gift of yourself to God and man." No person can naturally give this gift. Only as he surrenders to the Holy Spirit can he give this gift. And this is what it means to be filled or controlled by the Holy Spirit.

If a person is truly filled with the Holy Spirit, he will make love as a way of life. My favorite marriage counselor is Dr. Gary Chapman, whom I have known some 20 years. His book, *The Five Love Languages* is a classic on the subject of relationships in marriage. *The Five Love Languages* has sold more than four million copies in the USA and been translated into thirty-five languages around the world.

In his latest book, *Love as a way of Life,* Gary has shown how love is the key to the transformation of every aspect of life. He names seven characteristics of a loving person:

1. Kindness – Discovering the joy of helping others.

2. Patience – Accepting the imperfections of others.

3. Forgiveness – Finding freedom from the grip of anger.

4. Courtesy – Treating others as friends.

5. Humility – Stepping down so someone else can step up.

6. Generosity – Giving yourself to others.

7. Honesty – Revealing really who you are.

Gary concludes his book by showing how these seven characteristics transform:

a. Marriages

b. Parenting

c. The Workplace

When you ponder these seven characteristics of love, you immediately see that they cannot flow from our fleshly nature, which is self-serving. These traits can only come from the person who is born of the Holy Spirit "for everyone who loves (agape) is born of God and knoweth God" (1 John 4:7).

It is easy to say you are Spirit-filled. Many do who live totally self-centered lives. If you would know whether or not you are filled with the Holy Spirit, do this: On a scale of one to ten, with ten being the highest, rank yourself on how well you've shown the following characteristics:

I. To Your Spouse: (1-10)

1. Kindness _____
2. Patience _____
3. Forgiveness _____
4. Courtesy _____
5. Humility _____
6. Generosity _____
7. Honesty _____

II. To Your Children (1 -10)

1. Kindness _____
2. Patience _____
3. Forgiveness _____
4. Courtesy _____
5. Humility _____
6. Generosity _____
7. Honesty _____

III. To Your Co-workers (1-10)

1. Kindness _____
2. Patience _____
3. Forgiveness _____
4. Courtesy _____
5. Humility _____
6. Generosity _____
7. Honesty _____

Now ask yourself this question: am I Spirit-filled?

Dangerous and often damnable errors concerning the Holy Spirit

1. A Ghost – In 1611 ghost meant spirit, but a ghost today is a very bad critter hovering over a grave yard or haunted house.

2. A good feeling – emotionally

3. A good feeling – Physically – Ex. Tingle up the spine

4. Loud and noisy – Sometimes He is. Illustration: Fire fell at 16th Baptist Church, Greensboro, North Carolina in 1955. But more often the Holy Spirit manifests Himself by a "still small voice." Illustration: I was in a prayer meeting in Trinity Methodist church, Greensboro, North Carolina, 1958, when a "holy hush" came over us until I could not speak for a time, and turning to my dear friend Roy Putnam and said, "Please pray for me," and he replied, "I can't afford to, I must pray for myself."

5. Speaking through vocal chords – Never has He spoken to me through the English language. However, I was called to my largest and longest pastorate when the Holy Spirit spoke to a brother who had just heard me preach on the Holy Spirit, saying in the English language, "The man you just heard preach should pastor the First Baptist Church, Fort Smith, Arkansas." Whereupon, he notified the Search Committee of that church and the church called me as pastor where I served as pastor for almost twenty years. Never before or after have I known of the Holy Spirit speaking in vocal chords to any person but only in the "still small voice."

6. That He can be used and manipulated – The only predictable thing that the Holy Spirit is that He is unpredictable, except He always glorifies Jesus, not Himself, and speaks in accord with the Bible.

7. That you "get the Holy Spirit." For example, I have heard some say, "I was saved years ago but just 'got the Holy Ghost.'" Wrong. Acts 19:2; Romans 8:9b.

8. That you can be saved without the Holy Spirit. Wrong. John 3:5; Romans 8:9b; 1 Cor. 6:19-20.

9. That you can live the Christian life without the Holy Spirit. Illus: Galatians made this mistake (Gal. 3:1).

10. Separating the Holy Spirit from Jesus (John 14:18).

11. That you can do anything spiritually without the Holy Spirit. Illustration: During the days of His flesh, Jesus said to His followers "Without me you all can do nothing." (John 15:5). But when Jesus ascended to heaven, He commissioned the Holy Spirit to carry on His work in His place. So today we can truthfully say "Without the Holy Spirit, we can do nothing."

12. 12 things you cannot do without the Holy Spirit:

    (1) Be saved – John 3:5

    (2) Know you are saved – Romans 8:16

    (3) Understand the Bible – 1 Cor. 2:14

    (4) Pray – Romans 8:26

    (5) Worship – John 4:24

    (6) Witness – Acts 1:8

    (7) Bear godly fruit – Gal. 5:22-23

    (8) Have hope and joy – Romans 15:13

    (9) Overcome sin and the flesh – Romans 8:13

    (10) Have boldness – Acts 4:31

    (11) Preach or teach – 1 Cor. 2:3-4

    (12) Possess real joy – Acts 2:47

Five Positions On The Miraculous Gifts Of The Holy Spirit

The evangelical world is divided into five camps regarding their views of the operation of miraculous gifts of the Holy Spirit in the church today. Dr. Wayne Grudem, professor of theology at Trinity Evangelical Seminary, Deerfield, Illinois, summarizes the five views as follows, concluding with this statement, "I THINK WHAT PEOPLE REALLY WANT IS TO BE IN THE PRESENCE OF GOD." (Are Miraculous Gifts for Today, p. 347)

1. The CESSATIONIST Position:

The cessationist position argues that there are no miraculous gifts of the Holy Spirit today. Gifts such as prophecy, tongues, and healing were confined to the first century, and were used at the time the apostles were establishing the churches and the New Testament was not yet complete. This is a well-defined and often-defended position within evangelical scholarship.

There are cessationists within both the Reformed and the dispensational segments of evangelicalism. Reformed cessationism is represented by many of the faculty at Westminster Seminary, especially Richard Gaffin. Dispensational cessationists hold similar positions on this question but are in different institutions; they are represented by institutions such as Dallas Seminary and The Master's Seminary. Within the Lutheran tradition, conservative groups such as the Missouri Synod also hold mostly to a cessationist position.

Standing in clear opposition to the cessationist position are three groups that encourage the use of all spiritual gifts today: Pentecostals, charismatics, and the Third Wave. Although sometimes people have used the terms "Pentecostal" and "charismatic" indiscriminately to refer to all of there groups, the terms are more accurately understood in the following way:

2. **The PENTECOSTAL Position:**

Pentecostal refers to any denomination or group that traces its historical origin back to the Pentecostal revival that began in the United States in 1901, and that holds the following doctrines: (1) All the gifts of the Holy Spirit mentioned in the New Testament are intended for today; (2) baptism in the Holy Spirit is an empowering experience subsequent to conversion and should be sought by Christians today; and (3) when baptism in the Holy Spirit occurs, people will speak in tongues as a "sign" that they have received this experience. Pentecostal groups usually have their own distinct denominational structures, among which are the Assemblies of God, the Church of God in Christ, and many others.

3. **The CHARISMATIC Position:**

Charismatic, on the other hand, refers to any groups (or people) that trace their historical origin to the charismatic renewal movement of the 1960s and 1970s and that seek to practice all the spiritual gifts mentioned in the New Testament (including prophecy, healing, miracles, tongues, interpretation, and distinguishing between spirits). Among charismatics there are differing viewpoints on whether baptism in the Holy Spirit is subsequent to conversion and whether speaking in tongues is a sign of baptism in the Spirit. Charismatics by and large have refrained from forming their own denominations, but view themselves as a force for renewal within existing Protestant and Roman Catholic churches. There is no representative charismatic denomination in the United States today, but the most prominent charismatic spokesman is probably Pat Robertson with his Christian Broadcasting Network, the television program "The 700 Club," and Regent University (formerly CBN University).

4. **The THIRD WAVE Position:**

In the 1980's a third renewal movement arose, a movement called *The Third Wave* by missions professor C. Peter Wagner at Fuller Seminary (he referred to the Pentecostal renewal as the first wave of the Holy Spirit's renewing work in the modern church, and the charismatic movement as the second wave). Third Wave people encourage the equipping of all believers to use New Testament spiritual gifts today and say that the proclamation of the gospel should ordinarily be accompanied by "signs, wonders, and miracles," according to the New Testament pattern. They teach, however, that baptism in the Holy Spirit happens to all Christians at conversion and that subsequent experiences are better called "fillings" or "empowerings" with the Holy Spirit. Though they believe the gift of tongues exists today, they do not emphasize it to the extent that Pentecostals and charismatics do. The most prominent representative of the "Third Wave" is John Wimber, the late pastor of the Vineyard Christian Fellowship in Anaheim, California, and leader of the Association of Vineyard Churches.

5. **The OPEN BUT CAUTIOUS Position:**

There is yet another position, held by a vast number of evangelicals who think of themselves as belonging to none of these groups. These people have not been convinced by the cessationist arguments that relegate certain gifts to the first century, but they are not really convinced by the doctrine or practice of those who emphasize such gifts today either. They are open to the possibility of miraculous gifts today, but they are concerned about the possibility of abuses that they have seen in groups that practice these gifts. They do not think speaking in tongues is ruled out by Scripture, but they see many modern examples as not conforming to scriptural guidelines; some also are concerned that it often leads to divisiveness and negative results in churches today. They think churches should emphasize evangelism, Bible study, and faithful obedience as keys to personal and church growth, rather than miraculous gifts. Yet they appreciate some of the benefits that Pentecostal, charismatic, and Third Wave churches have brought to the evangelical world, especially a refreshing contemporary tone in worship and a challenge to renewal in faith and prayer. The "Open but Cautious Position" is the one held by the majority of evangelicals today.

The renewal of interest in the gifts of the Holy Spirit is perhaps the most encouraging development of our time. Why? Because it says that God's people are tired of religion without reality and hunger for the reality of the living God in their lives. I agree with Dr. Grudem, "What people really want is to be in the presence of God." Brother Pastors, you and I must see to it that this hunger of our people is met through our ministry to them. If we do so, the church faces its most glorious future. If not, churches by the thousand face their demise. You and I hold the answer.

How Does All This Affect Our Personal Ministries?

1. The Local Church – Each pastor should search the New Testament and decide his position on the miraculous gifts. Then he should fully explain his position to his people and specify in writing the policy he would follow in the church. For instance – how he would handle speaking in tongues, words of prophecy, etc.

2. Inter-denominational (ecumenical) meetings – In such meetings essentials which unify must be stressed, not the matters about which

there are disagreements. All evangelicals agree on the authority of the Word, the deity of Jesus, salvation by grace, etc., but not on such matters as tongues, words of prophecy, the ordinances of baptism and the Lord's supper, church government, details of the second coming, etc. The rule has long been stated "In essentials, unity; in non-essentials, liberty, and in all things charity."

I preside over a city wide inter-denominational prayer group which meets every Tuesday, 6 AM-7 AM. This prayer group began meeting in April 1999 and has continued to the present time. I suspect that all five views have been represented in our meetings – the Cessationists, Pentecostals, Charismatics, Third Wave and Open-but-Cautious. Great unity has marked our fellowship because we have stressed our likenesses, not our differences.

Chapter 3

Intimacy with the Father through Prayer

No person will ever conform to the "image of Christ" apart from having a meaningful time with God daily in prayer. It may be trite but it is tritely true that "You can do more than pray after you have prayed, but you can never do more than pray until you have first prayed." Thus prayer should be the top priority in every believer's life, for it is out of one's personal relationship with the Father that one finds strength to live a victorious life and to minister effectively. Jesus Himself said that men "should always pray and not give up," (Luke 18:1), meaning that if one does not constantly pray he will lose heart and live a defeated life out of his flesh. Therefore, I believe that the "one thing" every child of God should do is the very same "one thing" David said he was seeking. "One thing I have desired of the Lord, that will I seek after, that I may dwell in the house of the Lord all the days of my life, to behold His beauty and inquire in His tabernacle" (Psalm 27:4). Robert Murray McCheyne lived only 29 years, but impacted the world as few men have. His "Memoirs" is one of the most valuable books in my library of 10,000 volumes. Of prayer he wrote, "A calm hour with God is worth a lifetime with man."

I have struggled all my live to learn more about prayer, and the greatest single truth I ever learned is this: "When we work, we work, but when we pray, God works." Years ago a whole book was written on the subject, *They Found the Secret*. This book simply recounts the experiences of 20 ordinary guys who discovered life's greatest secret in my judgment, namely, that prayer brings into our lives all "the good things" God has for us (Matthew 7:11), the best being the fullness of the Holy Spirit, which Jesus promised comes through prayer (Luke 11:13).

Charles Steinmetz, a great discoverer and a greater Christian, was asked the question, "Mr. Steinmetz, what is the next great discovery man needs to make?" And he replied, "The thing we need to discover above all is "Prayer." Since prayer is absolutely indispensable for those who would be conformed to the image of Christ and who would serve him effectively, it must not be left to our convenience, moods or feelings.

We have got to understand that the best way to experience spiritual power, direction, and purpose is to have a meaningful time with God daily.

The number one priority in the life of a true disciple should be having a meaningful time with God daily. If nothing else gets done in your day, this must get done.

Seven guidelines for having this meaningful time:

1. A Special Time – "The first guideline to having a meaningful time with God daily is to have a special time that you meet with Him. It is your most important appointment, and you need to make and keep it daily. Ask yourself right now, 'What time am I going to meet with God every single day for the rest of my life?' Since this is the number one priority in the life of a true disciple, I believe that your appointment with God should take place before anything else in your life.

Your time with God should take place before you read the newspaper each day. It should take place before you turn on the television to watch your favorite newscast. Since a meaningful time with God is imperative for you to have a vital relationship with God, then the priorities of your day should reflect this truth. The moment you wander around the house or leave for work or school in the morning without having a meaningful time with God, you make yourself vulnerable to attacks from the enemy."[11]

"Some of you may protest, 'I am not a morning person.' Even if you are not a morning person by nature, it is still important for you to make your time with God the first thing every day. When you meet with God, it shows you depend upon Him. When you do not, it shows you depend upon yourself. If you are going to be involved in effective praying – talking to God and listening to what He is saying

---

[11] Dr. Ronnie Floyd, How To Pray, (Nashville: Word Publishing, 1999). p. 33.

– then you must set aside a time for this to happen, or else it will probably not happen."[12]

I have a time set aside for God. I meet God for a private devotion at 3:00 or 3:30 every morning. Yes, the Holy Spirit is awake at this time.

2. Sufficient Time – There is a place for short, even an "arrow" prayer. Jesus often prayed one sentence. But if you have a meaningful time with God, you must take some time. Jesus chided His disciples for not praying one hour. I recommend you begin with thirty minutes, move to one hour, and often you will need to tarry longer. Jesus commanded persistence in prayer if we expect to get answers (Matt. 7:7; Luke. 11:8). Persistence means time. How do you think God feels when we give Him no more than 2, 3, 4, 5 or 10 minutes in prayer? How much time are you praying daily?

3. A Special Place – "Places are important to God. All through Scripture, we read various accounts of God's activity, and often the place of the activity receives special attention. If you are going to have a meaningful time with God every day, then set aside a special place to meet with Him. This special place needs to be somewhere you enjoy. It needs to be somewhere private. The fewer interruptions you have, the easier it is for you to have a meaningful time with God.

I meet with God every morning in my study at home. This is my special place to be with Him. He has been so real to me in this place. He has spoken to me through His Word. He has built me back up when I have been discouraged. He has put me back together when I am broken. Yes, it is a special place—not because of the color of the room, the beauty of the desk, or the books on the shelves. The thing that makes it really special is that is where God and I hang out together."[13]

4. A Special Plan – "If you do not have a plan to meet with God and pray, then you probably will not do either one. If you are going to have a meaningful time with God daily, you need to develop a game plan. Every day is game day for the Christian. There are no off days or off seasons. In order to be ready for your game day every day, you need to follow a plan when you meet with God."[14]

---

[12] Ibid. p. 34
[13] Ibid. pp. 34-35
[14] Ibid. p. 35

I have used several prayer plans. I began with the Lord's Prayer, then the One Year Bible,[15] the ACTS (Adoration, Confession, Thanksgiving, Suffocation), then one chapter each day, Monday through Friday. Sometimes I combine plans. "Just remember this, if you do not plan to pray, you will not pray. In order to be an effective prayer warrior, you need to plan to meet with God daily."[16]

5. A Special Book – "The special book that you need to read is a compilation of sixty-six smaller books…This book is called the Bible. The Bible is essential for your life. It needs to be studied. It needs to be memorized. It needs to be read daily.

   There is no way that you can have a meaningful time with God without reading the Bible daily. The Bible is the main way God speaks to you. The Bible is His love letter to you. God's Word is intended to be a lamp for our feet and a light for our path. This kind of guidance is possible when you read it and study it during a daily time with Him."[17] It is by hearing the Bible that faith arises in our hearts (Rom. 10:17).

6. A Special Spirit – A special time, a sufficient time, a special place, a special plan, a special book—none of these will result in a meaningful time with the Lord unless you possess a special spirit. What is that spirit? A broken spirit and a contrite heart. This is the sacrifice God requires. This is the sacrifice He honors (Ps. 51:16-17). God dwells in only two places: in heaven and in a humble heart (Is. 57:15). He dwells through the Holy Spirit, the mediator of Jesus, in the humble spirit. But He mediates only with the humble spirit. "God resists the proud but gives grace to the humble" (1 Pt. 5:5 and James 4:6).

   You must have His effectual indwelling to have a meaningful time with the Lord, and you have it only if you approach Him with a repentant and broken heart.

7. A Special Hunger for God – We know it is God's will for us to have a hunger for Him (Matt.5:6 and John 7:37). If you don't have a hunger, you can pray and He will give it to you according to 1 John 5:14. What sends you to the refrigerator day and night? Hunger for food. Hunger for God will also send you to Him to pray daily.

---

[15] For example, *see One Year Bible: The New International Version* (Wheaton, IL: Tyndale, 1986).
[16] Dr. Ronnie Floyd, p. 36
[17] Ibid. p. 36

Ten Requirements For Answered Prayer

1. To Get Your Prayers Answered, You Must Pray in Jesus Name (John 14:14).

   When you pray in the name of Jesus, you are praying to the God who manifest Himself in Jesus. You are not praying to Allah or Buddha or some pantheistic force. Pastor Bob Russell was asked not to pray in Jesus name at a civic event. He ended his prayer "in the name of the Lion of Judah." After praying he thought to himself, "I am so clever, how smart I am." Then the Lord convicted him that he was shrewd but was a coward. "Jesus said, if you are ashamed of me and my words, I will be ashamed of you."[18]

   When you pray in Jesus name you are praying to the only way to God. This is clearly stated in 1 Timothy 2:5, "For there is one God and one Mediator between God and men, the Man Christ Jesus,"

2. To Get Your Prayers Answered, You Must Pray According to God's Will.

   When you pray in the name of the Lord, you are submitting your will to His will. You are acknowledging that if both parties don't agree, you want God's will to prevail. Bob Russell states, "We don't dictate to God what He is supposed to do. As Jesus Himself prayed in Gethsemane, so we should pray, 'Not my will, but Yours be done.'"[19]

3. To Get Your Prayers Answered, you must pray with dependence upon the Holy Spirit.

   Romans 8:26 is a special promise. "Likewise the Spirit also helps in our weaknesses. For we do not know what we should pray for as we ought, but the Spirit Himself makes intercession for us with groanings which cannot be uttered." Often we really don't know what to pray for, but when you sincerely pray in Jesus name, the Holy Spirit intercedes for you. He knows you better than you know

---

[18] Adapted from Bob Russell, *When God Answers Prayer* (West Monroe, LA: Howard, 2003), 45-46.
[19] Bob Russell, *When God Answers Prayer* (West Monroe, LA: Howard, 2003), p. 48.

yourself. He brings your heart and God's heart together to make something happen that is agreeable to both parties.

4. To Get Your Prayers Answered, You Must Pray in Faith.

Mark 11:24, James 5:15 and Hebrews 11:6 all speak of the importance of faith. The Apostle James says that when we pray, we must believe and not doubt (James 1:6-8). Does that mean that if you have any doubts, your prayers will not be answered? No. In Mark 9:20-24 a father requested of Jesus that He heal his son and Jesus replied, "If you can believe, all things are possible to him who believes, but Lord help my unbelief." (said the man). Jesus did not refuse to help the man because he had doubts. He proceeded to heal the man. God does not require perfect faith, but sincere faith.

5. To Get Your Prayers Answered, You Must Be Righteous in Your Lifestyle.

James 5:16 says, "Confess your trespasses to one another, and pray for one another, that you may be healed. The effective, fervent prayer of a righteous man avails much," now consider the following.

You must have right relations with God – "Behold, the LORD's hand is not shortened, That it cannot save; Nor His ear heavy, That it cannot hear. But your iniquities have separated you from your God; And your sins have hidden His face from you, So that He will not hear" (Is. 59:1-2).

You must have right relations with your fellow man – "If someone says, I love God, and hates his brother, he is a liar; for he who does not love his brother whom he has seen, how can he love God whom he has not seen? And this commandment we have from Him: that he who loves God must love his brother also" (1 John 4:20-21).

"Therefore if you bring your gift to the altar, and there remember that your brother has something against you, leave your gift there before the altar, and go your way. First be reconciled to your brother, and then come and offer your gift" (Matt. 5:23-24).

If you are at odds with another Christian, if you are at odds with God, you are not ready to pray. Go and make things right with your brother and then pray. Confessing your sins does not mean spilling your guts to everyone or airing your dirty laundry in public. Warren Wiersbe offered words of wisdom: "We must never confess sin beyond the circle of that sin's influence. Private sin requires private confession; public sin requires public confession. It is wrong for Christians to hang dirty wash in public, for such confessing might do more harm than the original sin."[20]

6. To Get Your Prayers Answered, You Must Pray Fervently.

"Confess your trespasses to one another, and pray for one another, that you may be healed. The effective, fervent prayer of a righteous man avails much" (James 5:16)

"Therefore I say to you, whatever things you desire when you pray, believe that you receive them, and you will have them" (Mark 11:24).

Just mumbling some words with no passion and sometimes half asleep will not be honored by God.

Permit me to give you three practical suggestions for praying with greater fervency.

*   Kneeling. It is nearly impossible to sleep when on your knees and harder for your mind to wander.

*   Pray aloud. When you pray aloud, you impress your spirit and keep your focus.

*   Fast. Fasting demonstrates your seriousness. Fasting reminds you that spiritual things are more important than physical things.

7. To Get Your Prayers Answered, You Must Persist in Prayer.

Luke 11:5-8 and Matthew 7:7: "And He said to them, "Which of you shall have a friend, and go to him at midnight and say to him, 'Friend, lend me three loaves; for a friend of mine has come to me on his journey, and I have nothing to set before him'; and he will answer from within and say, 'Do not trouble me; the door is now shut, and my children are with me in bed; I cannot rise and give to you'? I say to you, though he will not rise and give to him because he is his friend, yet because of his persistence he will rise and give him as many as *he needs*." "Ask, and it will be given to you; seek, and you will find; knock, and it will be opened to you." The words *ask, seek* and *knock* are in the present tense which means keep on asking, seeking and knocking. Russell states, "Don't quit praying

---

[20] Quoted in Russell, pp. 51-52.

just because your prayers aren't answered on the first request."[21] Jesus said, "Men ought always to pray and not give up" (Luke 18:1). Remember that God's delays are not His denials but a display of His grace. Isaiah 30:18 says "Therefore the LORD will wait, that He may be gracious to you; And therefore He will be exalted, that He may have mercy on you. For the LORD is a God of justice; Blessed are all those who wait for Him."

8. To Get Your Prayers Answered, You Must Pray With Boldness.

You are invited to pray boldly in Hebrews 4:16. Russell says he memorized the words of John Newton regarding asking largely of God, "Thou art coming to a King, large petitions with thee bring, for His grace and power are such, none can ever ask too much."[22] It is alleged that D. L. Moody prayed for $50,000 when the pastor suggested $5, and received $50,000.

9. To Get Your Prayers Answered, You Must

Incorporate Thanksgiving into Your Petitions "Be anxious for nothing, but in everything by prayer and supplication, with thanksgiving, let your requests be made known to God; and the peace of God, which surpasses all understanding, will guard your hearts and minds through Christ Jesus" (Phil. 4:6-7). With all your groaning, shove in a few Hallelujahs and Thanksgivings.

10. To Get Your Prayers Answered, You Must Abide in God's Word

"If you abide in Me, and My words abide in you, you will ask what you desire, and it shall be done for you" (John. 15:7)

"One who turns away his ear from hearing the law, Even his prayer is an abomination" (Proverbs28:9).

A Personal Prayer Plan

Prayer must not be left to convenience, our feelings or our moods. The command of our Lord is to pray continually (Luke 18:1) and persistently (Luke 18:5-12). He, Himself, prayed several hours per day before the light of day (Mark 1:35). I believe every believer should also pray continually, persistently, and prior to daybreak if possible.

---

[21] Ibid. 63.
[22] Ibid., 67.

52

One fact is well attested: No one will ever have a powerful prayer life unless he plans it. Left to convenience and feelings, you would do well to pray two hours per week.

Consider the following "Personal Prayer Plan."

1. **Step One: Read The Bible.**

   - Before you begin to read, bow your head, be quiet for a moment and clear your mind.

   - Then pray this prayer, "Dear Father, speak to me through your Word today."

   - Use the One Year Bible or some systematic plan.

   - Now take your time.

   - You may want to write meaningful verses in your notebook.

2. **Step Two: The Four "Talking Principles" Begin With The Letters – ACTS:**[23]

   Adore or praise the Lord. Praise is your adoration for Him who loves you so much.

   Confess. Sin clogs the lines of communication between you and God. Claim the promise of 1 John 1:9 which says, "If we confess our sins, He is faithful and just to forgive us our sins and to cleanse us from all unrighteousness." Also Proverbs 28:13, "He who covers his sins will not prosper, But whoever confesses and forsakes them will have mercy."

   Thanksgiving. Thanksgiving is a verbal expression to God for all He has done for you. Be specific. "In everything give thanks; for this is the will of God in Christ Jesus for you" (1 Thess. 5:18).

   Supplication. This is petition and intercession.

   - Focus your prayer on personal needs (petition).

   - Stand in the gap between God and the person for whom you pray (intercession).

   - One may also use the Lord's Prayer.

---

[23] Bill Bright, *The Coming Revival,*(Orlando, Florida: Newlife Publications, 1995) p. 188.

3. **Step Three: Weekly Prayer Calendar.**

In order not to miss important objects of prayer, you will need to organize your prayer according to the days of the week. The following is an example:

Sunday – World Missions, Evangelism, Missionaries. Your praying is part of your vital involvement in world evangelization And Jesus came and spoke to them, saying, "All authority has been given to Me in heaven and on earth. Go therefore and make disciples of all the nations, baptizing them in the name of the Father and of the Son and of the Holy Spirit, teaching them to observe all things that I have commanded you; and lo, I am with you always, even to the end of the age." Amen (Matt. 28:18-20).

Monday – United States of America, The President, your Congressman, Senators, Mayor, Governor, etc. You are to "pray for all men in authority" (1 Tim. 2:1-2), regardless of whether you agree with them or not. "Therefore I exhort first of all that supplications, prayers, intercessions, and giving of thanks be made for all men, for kings and all who are in authority, that we may lead a quiet and peaceable life in all godliness and reverence."

Tuesday – The lost, unchurched, lost people in China, India, the Middle East, Europe, the USA and around the world (Rom. 10:1). "Brethren, my heart's desire and prayer to God for Israel is that they may be saved."

Wednesday – Friends.

Thursday – Christian Leaders of the nations and world.

Friday – Relatives.

Saturday – Local churches and pastors.[24]

There are two Urgent Categories of Prayer: 1) Urgent Current Needs – There are always immediate critical needs that require daily prayer; and 2) Continuing Needs – There are always critical needs which never cease to be needs, such as prayer for your children by name, for the Holy Spirit's infilling, for the boldness to witness daily.

---

[24] Quoted in Ronnie Floyd, *How to Pray,* (Nashville, Tennessee: Word Publishers, 1955), pp. 217-219.

4. Step Four: Journal.

I say to my students "Anything worth speaking is worth writing down." Also, anything worth praying is worth writing down. I regret that I have not done this through the years.

My nervousness, mobility, and unending labors have prevented this. Also, I have depended on my God-blessed memory, but no mind can recall everything. I have a friend, Ronnie Floyd, who closes his prayer time by writing a one-page letter to God. This letter records his main burdens of that day and also the joy of answered prayer.

5. Step Five: Pray it through.

Some years ago the word circulated that if one asked God more than once he was showing his lack of faith. This teaching is totally contrary to the teaching of Jesus. Jesus commands us "To ask and keep on asking." "Seek and keep on seeking." "Knock and keep on knocking" (Luke 11:9 and Matt. 7:7). Jesus illustrates this truth by telling of an unwilling neighbor who gave his friend bread simply because he kept on asking, seeking and knocking. Woodrow Kroll goes to the heart of the matter when he states, "If persistence was the key to the unwilling heart of a neighbor, how much more effective will persistence be to the willing heart of God."[25]

How long should you pray through? Ronnie Floyd says to pray until one of the following three things occur, and I agree: 1) Until you know it is not God's will; 2) until God answers your prayer; or 3) until God releases you.[26] I say, "Pray when you feel like it, pray when you don't feel like it and pray until you do feel like it." (Stephen Olford)

---

[25] Quoted in Ronnie Floyd, *How to Pray,* (Nashville, Tennessee: Word Publishers, 1955), p. 106.
[26] Ibid. pp. 106-109

Prayer Busters And How To Bust Them

If you are not getting your prayers answered, you should ask three questions:

1. Are my prayers right?
2. Is the timing right?
3. Am I right?

If constantly your prayers are not answered, it is unlikely that your prayers are wrong or that the timing is wrong. The major problem is probably you. So let's look at twelve prayer busters and how to bust the prayer busters:

The first prayer buster is *lostness*. Without a personal relationship with the Father, you cannot pray. Romans 10:13 says,…"whoever calls on the name of the LORD shall be saved." and in John 14:6, "Jesus said to him, "I am the way, the truth, and the life. No one comes to the Father except through Me." So it's clear that no man or woman comes to the Father except through Jesus. The answer is to get truly saved.

The second prayer buster is *prayerlessness*. Jesus said, "Ask and it shall be given" (Matt. 7:7). James spells it out further, "You have not because you ask not" (James 4:2). The answer is to begin praying and keep on praying no matter your discouragements.

The third prayer buster is *partial-praying*. Jesus said not only to "ask" but to "seek" and to "knock." Sometimes you can receive an answer by merely asking, but in most cases you must also "seek" and then "knock." I arise early to first ask; then I seek; and then I go to my office to knock. The answer is more time in prayer each day.

The fourth prayer buster is *heartless praying*. Just saying words is not praying. Prayer is passion, conviction, urgency and feeling (James 5:17-18 and Mark 11:24). The answer is to surrender to the Holy Spirit.

The fifth prayer buster is *unconfessed sin.* (Is. 59:1-2 and Ps. 66:18). The answer is true confession, not just naming your sins, but naming them personally and specifically and turning from them in the power of God (Prov. 28:13). "Lord, forgive me of my many sins" is a cop out. You must name your sins one by one and specifically, "Lord, I backbited Hazel Snodgrass today. I repent and ask your forgiveness and cleansing."

Broken Relationships "Therefore if you bring your gift to the altar, and there remember that your brother has something against you, leave your gift there before the altar, and go your way. First be reconciled to your brother, and then come and offer your gift" (Matt. 5:23-24). John states, "If you say you walk in light and hate your brother you are still in darkness" (1 John 2:9). The answer is to seek reconciliation. It may not be possible but we must try. "If it is possible, as much as depends on you, live peaceably with all men" (Romans 12:18).

Mistreating your spouse (1 Pet. 3:7). The answer is to obey Eph. 5:25 which says, "Husbands, love your wives, just as Christ also loved the church and gave Himself for her,"

Uncaring Attitude toward the oppressed (Prov. 21:13). "Whoever shuts his ears to the cry of the poor will also cry himself and not be heard." The answer is to ask forgiveness and repent and start helping the oppressed.

Stingy heart (Luke 16:11). "Therefore if you have not been faithful in the unrighteous mammon, who will commit to your trust the true riches?" The answer is to start tithing and giving as a way of life. Claim the promise of Luke 6:38. "Give, and it will be given to you: good measure, pressed down, shaken together, and running over will be put into your bosom. For with the same measure that you use, it will be measured back to you."

Bad Motives (James 4:3). "You ask and do not receive, because you ask amiss, that you may spend it on your pleasures." Many good prayers go unanswered because of their selfish motives. The answer is to check your prayers by four questions:

* Does this prayer glorify Jesus Christ?

* Does this prayer help carry out the Great Commission?

* Does this prayer build the local church?

* And does this prayer build the kingdom and help me spiritually?

Hostility toward the Word of God (Prov. 28:9). "One who turns away his ear from hearing the law, Even his prayer is an abomination." The answer is to search your soul to see if you are saved. Repent. Get back under the Word. Read it. Hear it on every occasion possible, internalize it and obey it.

Unbelief. (Heb. 11:6). "But without faith it is impossible to please Him, for he who comes to God must believe that He is, and that He is a rewarder of those who diligently seek Him." The answer is a steady dose of the Word, answered prayer, and close contact with those walking in victory.

Do you have to be sinlessly perfect or possessing flawless faith? No, but Psalms 66:18 must be taken seriously, "If I regard iniquity in my heart, The Lord will not hear." In 1981 Doris and I were asked by the International Mission Board of the SBC to go to Thailand to minister to our missionaries. Upon arriving we learned that the President of the Thai Convention, Brother Bonkramp, had terminal cancer. After two days of praying we felt led, at his invitation, to pray for his healing. We did so in faith and, believing God had directed us to do so, but at the same time doubting that he would live at that point. About a year later, we were surprised when he appeared at our church to attend our annual clinic on evangelism. When asked how he was doing, he exclaimed victoriously, "After you prayed for me, I was healed." So God honored our prayer, not because our faith was perfect, but it was earnest, sincere and obedient.

Collateral Material For The Third "I"
What Moves Us To Make Prayer The Priority Of Our Lives

Prayer should be the #1 priority of every Christian, but it is not with most Christians. What, then, moves a Christian to make prayer the priority of his or her life? I believe there are seven paramount and compelling movers to pray:

I. **A Realization of The Greatness of God** – His total sufficiency to meet every human need. A. W. Tozer said, "What we believe about God is the most important thing about us." Certainly when it comes to prayer, the concept we have of God determines our praying. Our belief or lack of it translates into our attitudes and actions concerning prayer. Corrie Ten Boom said, "The size of our prayers is determined by the size of our God." If our God is big, our prayers will be big, but if our God is little, our prayers will be little and anemic. Illus: Rabbi Kushner wrote a best seller, *Why Bad Things Happen to Good People*, in which he says God wants to answer all our prayers and meet every need, but He is not able to do so under many circumstances. How much praying do you think people will do who believe in such a limited God?

- Illus: Many times as I have struggled in prayer I have found it very helpful to review in my mind the greatness of God (His total sufficiency under all circumstances) by recalling His Names in the Old Testament:

1. **Jehovah Raah** – "The God who sees" (Gen 16:13)

2. **Jehovah Ropha** – "The God who heals" (Exodus 15:26)

3. **El Elyon** – "God the Most High" (Gen. 14:22). Notice its use in connection with Lucifer's desire to be like the Most High (Is. 14:14)

4. **El Olam** – "The everlasting God" (Gen. 21:33). Notice this use in connection with God's inexhaustible strength (Is. 40:28).

5. **El Shaddai** – "The Almighty God" (Gen 17:1). This probably derives from a related word which means "mountain" and pictures God as the overpowering Almighty One standing on a mountain. The name is often used in connection with the chastening of God's people, as in Ruth 1:20-21 and the thirty-one times it is used in the book of Job.

6. **Jehovah Jireh** – The Lord provides (Gen 22:14). This is the only occurrence in the Bible. After the angel of the Lord pointed to a ram as a substitute for Isaac, Abraham named the place, "the Lord provides."

7. **Jehovah Nissi** – The Lord is my Banner (Ex. 17:15). Similarly, after the defeat of the Amalekites, Moses erected an altar and called it "Yahweh Nissi." Actually this and the other compounds are not really names of God, but designations that grew out of commemorative events.

8. **Jehovah Shalom** – The Lord is peace (Judges 6:24).

9. **Jehovah Sabbaoth** – "The Lord of hosts" (1 Sam 1:3) The hosts are the angels of heaven which are ready to obey the Lord's commands. This title was often used by the prophets (Isaiah and Jeremiah) during times of national distress to remind the people that Yahweh was still their Protector.

10. **Jehovah Maccaddeshcem** – The Lord thy Sanctifier (Ex. 31:13).

11. **Jehovah Roi** – "The Lord…my shepherd" (Psalm 23:1).

12. **Jehovah Tsidkenu** – The Lord our Righteousness (Jer. 23:6). This title was a direct thrust against King Zedekiah (which means Yahweh is righteousness) who was a completely unrighteous king (2 Ch. 36:12-13).

13. **Jehovah Shammah** – "The Lord is there" (Eze. 48:35).

14. **Jehovah Elohim Israel** – "The Lord God of Israel" (Judges 5:3). This is a designation frequently used by the prophets (Is. 17:6), similar to the God of Abraham, Isaac and Jacob.

15. **Qadosh Israel** - "The Holy One of Israel" (Is. 1:4).

- **The "Great I Am's" Concerning Jesus in the Gospel of John:**

1. John 6:35 – I am the bread of life.

2. John 8:12 – I am the light of the world.

3. John 10:9 – I am the door.

4. John 10:11 – I am the good shepherd.

5. John 11:25 – I am the resurrection and the life

6. John 14:6 – I am the way, the truth, and the life

7. John 15:1 – I am the vine

Prayer hinges on the confidence we have to whom we are praying, and that confidence is directly proportional to the greatness of God spelled out in His name.

II. **The Recognition of The Greatness of Our Needs** – Our total insufficiency in meeting them. Most people recognize at least some of their needs, and they think they have the ability to meet them, or some other human being can meet them. This explains why very few people, including most professing Christians, make prayer the number 1 priority in their lives. Thus the problem is pride (*hubris*), which St. Augustine called "the mother of all sins." The constitution of the Kingdom of God is the beatitudes, and the first beatitude states that entrance into the Kingdom of God is only for "the poor in spirit" (Matthew 5:3). The Greek had two words for "poor." One was *penes*, which means "needy." The other was *ptochos*, which meant "total bankruptcy." Such poverty is the door way into the Kingdom or salvation, and it is also the key to effective prayer. That is why "humility" must precede prayer if we expect our prayers to be effective. "If my people...will humble themselves first and then pray...then will I hear from heaven..." (2 Chron. 7:14).

III. **The Experience of Answered Prayer.** If one has experienced answered prayer, he will be moved to keep on praying because he knows prayer works. Statistics reveal that many people who once prayed quit because they said their prayers were not answered. Most of the latter were unbelievers, prayed unanswerable prayers, the timing was wrong, or they just quit praying before God chose to answer. The word of Jesus to Jarius and others was "Keep on Believing." I prayed for 33 years before my father-in-law was saved. Don't quit praying if your prayers have not been answered. Find out why, make corrections, and see your prayers answered. Answered prayers of the past will move your heart to pray in the present.

IV. **The Sheer Joy of Communicating With The Heavenly Father or Coming into His Presence.** "The joy of the Lord is our strength" (Neh. 8:10). There is no greater joy than being in the presence of God through prayer. "In thy presence is fullness of joy and at thy right hand there are pleasures forevermore" (Psalm 16:11). Those who experience this joy, even once, will be moved to experience it often. Such was David's highest desire. "One thing have I desired of the LORD, that will I seek after; that I may dwell in the house of the LORD all the days of my life, to behold the beauty of the LORD, and to enquire in his temple" Psalm 27:4).

V. **The Compelling Example of God's Love Demonstrated at Calvary.** "What shall we then say to these things. He who spared not His Son but delivered Him up for us all, how shall He not by Him give us all things" (Romans 8:31-32). The logic of those verses is irresistible: An all loving God, who has already given His very best, will not refuse to give us lesser things, provided we ask in prayer.

VI. **The Intercession of The Holy Spirit** to make up for our ignorance of God's perfect will when we pray (Romans 8:26). This shows how very important it is for us to be surrendered (filled or controlled) to the Holy Spirit. Thus God commands every believer not to grieve the Holy Spirit by sinning (Ephesians 4:30) nor quench (1 Thess. 5:19) Him (refuse to obey His leading), lest He become somewhat "dysfunctional" and cease His intercession for us.

One could meet all six requirements discussed above, but to make prayer a priority he would need one more thing:

VII. **Faith Strong Enough to Trust God to Meet Our Needs.** How do we get such faith? The Bible says real faith comes from hearing the Word of God. What does it mean to hear? To hear not just with our ears but to hear in our heart and souls with a desire to obey what we hear. Samuel cried out to God, "Speak Lord, for thy servant heareth." Samuel was not just pledging to God that he would hear sounds and words, but that he would hear God's message so he would know and obey that message. Millions sit in churches every Sunday and hear good messages and are never changed. Some hear and are radically changed. PTL.

But how can we hear the Word so that it will produce a trusting or surrendering faith? By just reading the Word? No. By just studying the Word? No. By hearing the Word taught or preached? No. By teaching and preaching ourselves? No.

1. We must *know* the Word in our head by diligent study.

2. We must *stow* the Word in our heart by memorization and meditation.

3. We must *show* the Word of God by obeying its teaching.

4. We must *sow* the Word of God by our witnesses.

   This is what we call "Internalizing the Word of God."

   So let us now "Internalize" some key verses on prayer:

1. Hebrews 11:6

2. Mark 11:24

3. Jeremiah 33:3

4. Matthew 21:22

Why God Desires That Prayer Be Our # 1 Priority

The Bible makes it clear that prayer should be the priority in the lives of His followers. Jesus prayed without ceasing (Mark 1:35) and commands the same for His children (Luke 18:1). Paul prayed without ceasing (Phil. 1:3-4) and commanded the same for us (1 Thess. 5:17). The early church was birthed through a ten-day prayer meeting (Acts 1:14) and in the Book of Acts we see believers always doing three things: *praying, praising*, and *witnessing* (Acts 8:4). When we read church history, we note that every effective servant of Jesus Christ made prayer the #1 priority in his life or her life. But why?

1. When Prayer is your priority, God is your priority and Jesus is Lord.

2. When Prayer is your priority, you show you are dependant upon God, not self.

3. When Prayer is your priority, you show that you are thinking of heavenly things, rather than materialistic and sensual matters (Col. 3:1-2).

4. When Prayer is your priority, you show you desire fellowship with God more than any other thing in your life (Psalm 27:4).

5. When Prayer is your priority, obedience to His Word is a priority. Example: the first Commandment and the Great Commandment.

6. When Prayer is your priority, you are protecting yourself from evil which may assault or tempt you (Matt. 6:9-13; Ephesians 6:18-19).

7. When Prayer is your priority, you are enabling yourself to do all the other things God requires of you (Romans 15:30).

8. When Prayer is your priority, you show that you have a living and genuine faith in God (Hebrews 11:6).

9. When Prayer is your priority, you become the recipient of all the marvelous benefits God promises but only through prayer. Jesus says, "Ask and it shall be given" (Matt. 7:7) but "You have not because you ask not" (James 4:2).

10. When Prayer is your priority, you demonstrate that you love Jesus with all your heart and hunger to be with Him above all. "A calm hour with God is worth a life time with man." (Robert McCheyne).

11. When Prayer is your priority, you have impossible and unthinkable and inexplicable blessings (Jer. 33:3; Ephesians 3:20).

12. When Prayer is your priority, it shows you have a personal, saving relationship with Jesus Christ (Psalm 27:4).

Benefits Which Come When Prayer Is A Priority:

1. Spiritual healing (salvation) – Rom. 10:13

2. Physical healing – James 5:14-16

3. Strength for daily living – Luke 18:1

4. Peace rather than worry – Phil. 4:6-7

5. Daily needs – food, clothing, shelter – Matthew 6:9-13; 6:33.

6. Freedom from fear – Psalm 34:4

7. Power for witnessing – Acts 4:31

8. The continual infilling of the Holy Spirit – Luke 11:13

9. Nearness to God – James 4:8

10. Protection from evil – Matthew 6:9-13

11. Prevention from burn-out – Luke 18:1

Illus: It is alleged that a certain man went to heaven. St. Peter escorted him into a large warehouse where he noted many unwrapped gifts lying on shelves. When he asked Peter what these gifts were for, he replied, "These were the many wonderful gifts God had for His children, but they never asked Him for them." How about you?

"What a man is: He is on his knees before God – nothing more and nothing less." (Robert Murray McCheyne).

The Three Stages Of Prayer

Charles Steinmetz, a great Christian Scientist and discoverer, was asked, "Mr. Steinmetz, what should be our next discovery?" To which he replied, "We need to discover prayer." How profound and spiritually instructing and how it resonates with my own experience. From my own experience I would say that the greatest growth I have undergone has been in the area of prayer. I like to think of this as my "progressive maturity" in my relationship and partnership with God.[27] Since I moved to Wilmington in 1993, I have experienced a dimension in prayer I never knew previously in fifty years of ministry. There are three stages of prayer through which I have passed: Biblical praying consists of more than three elements, but the three below describe my progress in discovering the growing depths of prayer.

1. **Prayer Stage # 1 – A simple childlike request for something.** This is a very vital part of prayer and a point where any born again person can begin. Why? Because prayer is a child talking to His father. One of the best books I ever read on prayer is titled, *"Prayer: Asking and Receiving,* by John R. Rice. In this book, the author likens prayer to your backing up a pick-up truck to a large warehouse and saying, "fill it up" with whatever you desire. Another way to put it is this: Prayer is a young guy going to a Burger King and ordering "A Whopper well-done, but hold the pickles and lettuce – with extra ketchup."

   I became strongly conscious of this kind of praying when I was 26 years old and joined a classmate of mine in Duke University in praying this prayer, "Lord, please have someone send me $100 so I can attend Campus in the Woods in Canada." To my amazement my friend, Ed Hackney, received exactly $100 within a few days. To make simple requests to God is a necessary part of prayer. Jesus used this method. He commands direct petition in the Lord's prayer (Matthew 6:9ff). Paul commands this – "Let your request be made known unto God" (Phil. 4:6). However, if one never moves beyond simple petition, he runs into grave danger of missing other dynamics in prayer (such as meditation

---

[27] Philip Yancy, *Prayer, Does it Make a Difference,* p. 106

and practicing the presence of the Lord) and looking upon prayer as a very selfish and self-serving act. Illus: Lord, bless me, my wife, my son Bill and his wife, us 4 and no more." So let's move on to another stage in prayer.

2. **Prayer Stage #2 – Meditation, or what some call "Keeping Company with God."**[28] We should move beyond mere request and make meditation our experience in prayer. Meditation is a vital and necessary part of prayer. Why? Because meditation can refine or even change our requests as we talk to God and seek His direction. Ultimately you want to pray for what God wants, and He may show you during meditation, that what you requested was not what He wanted at all. There is certainly no doubt that meditation adds a sweet dimension to prayer and gives you a great desire to meet with the Lord every day. However, meditation moves prayer from beyond requesting to a relationship which makes prayer enjoyable and exciting. A pastor friend of mine wrote a classic on prayer, in which he says, "Nothing lies beyond the reach of prayer, except that which lies outside the will of God." (Jack Taylor). It is often as we wait in meditation that we come to see God's will and see our prayers answered.

3. **Prayer Stage #3 – Submission to God's Will.** This stage of prayer has become very important to me in recent years. Jesus Himself makes simple requests to His Father in prayer and commands us to do the same (Mk. 11:24). Jesus also no doubt meditated as He prayed. But the climax of His praying was in the Garden of Gethsemane when He in agony said to His Father, "If possible, remove this cup from me; Nevertheless, not my will but yours be done" (Matthew 26:39). Strange as it may seem the Father did not answer that prayer of His Son, and there are times when He cannot answer our prayers which are contrary to His holy purposes and our personal good.

I think the highest experience in prayer comes when we learn that God has ordained prayer as a means of getting God's will done on earth, not ours. As one great scholar wrote, "Prayer is not overcoming God's reluctance but laying hold of God's highest willingness."

---

[28] Ibid. p. 107

Conclusion: Why not use the three stages of prayer in one prayer experience: For instance:

1. Make your request known to God.

2. Meditate on it and dialogue with God for fuller understanding and finally be willing to say to the Father,

3. Father, not my will, but yours be done.

Example: Last Monday, on Laborless Day, as I prayed, my heart being filled with my message to you today, I felt impressed to go through the three stages. First, I prayed that the Lord provide us a lot and building for MMM (Stage 1). Then I began to think and talk to God, asking if we really needed the building now and could we maintain it with our resources or should we wait on the Lord for this (Stage 2). Finally, I said to the Lord, "Not my will, but yours be done." (Stage 3). Will the Lord provide us a place? I cannot say so with eternal certainty, but I am absolutely convinced that He will, in His timing, for His ultimate glory, and the maximum benefit for MMM. *Soli Deo Gloria*.

Chapter 4

Intentional Involvement in the World Mission of Christ

The World Mission of Christ dictates that every follower of Christ would "go into all the world" and "make disciples of all nations" (Matthew 28:18-20; Mark 16:15; Luke 24:47-49; John 20:21b and Acts 1:8) Obedience to this commandment is not optional. Every born again individual is under orders of the risen Christ to carry out this Commission. His Commission is His final word to His people after His ascension – what I like to call "Our Orders from Headquarters."

Two questions arise relating to Christ's Great Commission?

1. **How can the individual carry out the Great Commission?** Someone has observed that there are four requirements for carrying out the Great Commission in the local church. (1) Genuine Care, (2) Intercessory Prayer, (3) Personal Affair, (4) Financial Share. Let us focus on the fourth requirement – Financial Share. While care, prayer, and personnel are absolutely required for the fulfillment of the Great Commission, finances are also indispensable. As Louis Evans said, "The water of life is free, but it takes money to buy pails to carry this water across the earth." Since finances are essential, the Lottie Moon Christmas Offering is crucial for our Foreign Mission enterprise in the Southern Baptist Convention. (Also Annie Armstrong offering for Home Missions). In fact we might say, as the Lottie Moon Christmas offering goes, so goes Foreign Missions in the Southern Baptist Convention. (I am not discounting the critical role of the Cooperative Program). I am advised that the Lottie Moon Christmas offering provides one-half of the budget of our International Mission Board. Therefore, if we can find a way to substantially increase the giving of our people to the Lottie Moon Christmas offering, we will enter into an exciting new day in our missionary outreach. I desire to share with you two things which I have done which dramatically increased the giving to the Lottie Moon Christmas offering in the churches I served:

1. Held the first Sunday in December – before the people spend all their money for Santa.

2. Church decorated in white. Beautiful Christmas tree erected at front of sanctuary decorated with chrismons.

3. Each member of Sunday School instructed one month in advance to bring *two gifts: A gift for local missions* wrapped in white, and labeled appropriately (ex. Socks for 5 year old girl) to be put under the Christmas tree. Also a *monetary gift* for Lottie Moon offering in Lottie Moon envelopes.

4. Each person sits with his or her Sunday School class in the worship service.

5. *Great Mission March* – Pastor preaches 12 minute sermon on The Great Commission. Then he calls the names of each class and leaders, beginning with the youngest. The people march down to deposit two gifts and return to their seats. The choir and congregation joyfully sing Christmas carols while the people come down. (Teachers provide gifts for anyone present who may not bring or cannot afford a gift).

The Mission Savings Club This idea jumped out at me one day as I read 1 Cor. 16:2 in the NIV. It reads like this, "On the first day of each week, each one of you should set aside a sum of money in keeping with his income…" When I saw the words, "set aside a sum of money each week," I thought of the "Christmas Savings Clubs" by which people set aside money for Christmas throughout the year. I then asked myself, "Why couldn't we have Mission Savings Clubs to set aside money for missions throughout the year?" I decided we should and could. In fact, I was compellingly convinced that the Holy Spirit was leading me to do so. I obeyed Him. Here's the way the Mission Savings Club works:

- Print on all offering envelopes the words, "Mission Savings Club," alongside General Fund, Building Fund, etc. Persons electing to give would mark the slot, "Mission Savings Club."

- Encourage your people to give a small offering through the church each week to the Lottie Moon Christmas offering above the tithe. Sometimes the gifts are no more than 50 cents or $1.00.

- Inform the people regularly what has been given toward the Lottie Moon goal. The annual goal is set and announced at the beginning of the budget year. I first used the Mission Savings Club in the First Baptist Church, Fort Smith, Arkansas. Our goal was $100,000 and by the time of White Christmas the church had given about half of this goal through the Mission Savings Club.

Results Of White Christmas And Mission Savings Club:

1. First Baptist Church, Fort Smith (8000 members). The Lottie Moon Christmas offering increased from $3,300.00 to $100,000.

2. Clifton Baptist (85 members) – Lottie Moon Christmas offering increased from $140.00 to $540.00 the first year.

3. Houston Northwest Baptist, Houston, Texas (3000 members) – Lottie Moon Christmas offering increased from $2,700.00 to $41,000 in three years.

4. First Baptist, Leland, NC (300 members) – Lottie Moon Christmas offering increased the first year from $1,800 to $10,200.

5. Calvary Baptist Church, Wilmington, NC (1700 members) – Lottie Moon Christmas offering increased the first year from $11,000 to $30,000.

If our churches would use the two above ideas, I am convinced that our mission offerings would quadruple or more within three years. If any church is afraid that Home Missions would be slighted by this arrangement, I would suggest that the offering in December include all missions. In Fort Smith I used the two ideas just for Foreign Missions and took special offerings for Home Missions. Home Missions was not hurt at all. However, in Houston, I included all missions in the special December emphasis. The WMU has historically promoted the Lottie Moon offering. They could still do this with my suggestions, with the added plus of having the pastors promoting missions throughout the church.

How does obedience to this Commission help to "conform us to the image of Christ," which is the sole purpose of Mentoring Men for the Master? The answer to this question is obvious. How could anyone expect to be "conformed to the image of Christ" or to be a true Christ-follower and not seek to win the lost for whom He died and for which He so clearly commands that we do the same.

Moreover, the sharing of our faith is a major factor in our spiritual growth. The Apostle Paul is bold to pray this prayer for every believer, "I pray that you may be active in sharing your faith that you may have a full understanding of all the good things he has in Christ." (Philemon 1:6 NIV). The Scripture promises that God gives the fullness of the Holy Spirit to those who obey Him (Acts 5:32b). This promise is for those who already have the Holy Spirit in them, thus meaning that there will be an overflow of the Holy Spirit in all who "make disciples" in the Name of Jesus; and the greatest gift of all is the Holy Spirit in all His fullness (Luke 11:13) Why? Because the Holy Spirit is the bringer of "all the spiritual blessings in the heavenly places in Christ." (Ephesians 1:3). The words translated, "spiritual blessings" *pneumatike*, mean all the things bestowed by the Holy Spirit, chief of which would be: the fruit of the Holy Spirit (Galatians 5:22-23), which is the character of Jesus Himself; the power of God to witness (Acts 1:8); the overflowing "joy and hope" of the Holy Spirit (Romans 15:13) victory over all indwelling sin (Romans 8:13); victory over the self life (Romans 8:13) and constant fellowship with the living Christ.

The truth of what I am saying is witnessed when anyone wins a soul to Christ. When he does, he is filled with joy, those around him rejoice, and when the saved person professes his salvation before the church, a spirit of revival sweeps the church. What a thrill to see a local church bubbling with the joy of the Holy Spirit because souls are being won by the members, and what a pitiable, even depressing experience to see a church as dead as a corpse when no soul winning is going on.

72

Collateral Material For The Fourth "I"

26 Vital Questions to Clarify the World Mission of Christ and Our Personal Responsibility in This Mission

1. **What is the "World Mission of Christ"?** The Father sent Jesus into the world "to seek and save that which is lost," (Luke 19:10) and after His resurrection from the dead Jesus commanded His followers to carry out the same mission. "As the Father has sent me into the world, so do I send you" (John 20:21b).

2. **Is the "World Mission of Christ" spelled out by Jesus in the New Testament?** Absolutely in 5 places in the New Testament: Matt. 28:18-20; Mark 16:15; Luke 24:47-49; John 20:21b; Acts 1:8.

3. **What are three imperatives in the Great Commission?**
    a. Make Disciples
    b. Mark Disciples
    c. Mature Disciples

4. **Who is responsible for carrying out the "World Mission of Christ"?** Every truly saved or born again individual. The Great Commission plainly commands, "Go ye or all of you go..."

5. **What is the geographical extent of our going?** Into all the world.

6. **Where should we start in carrying out the mission?** Acts 1:8 says the believer is to witness <u>Both</u> in Jerusalem, Judea, Samaria and to the ends of the earth, but to begin in Jerusalem.

7. **How can one living in Wilmington, N.C. carry out the Great Commission at the same time into all the world?**
    a. Pray urgently for missionaries around the world
    b. Tithe through your church.
    c. Be involved in a witnessing program in your church.
    d. Give to special mission offerings like Lottie Moon and Annie Armstrong.
    e. Make periodic trips to the mission field.
    f. Teach your children to be missionaries
    g. Become a career missionary if God leads.

8. **What is the purpose of the "World Mission of Christ"?** To win lost persons to a saving knowledge of Christ until they will openly confess their salvation before men and become a member of the "University of Christ," the local church.

9. **What is the ultimate purpose of the mission?** That those who are won may become soul-winners themselves. Notice these final words of the Great Commission, "Teaching them to obey all things I have commanded them" (Matt. 28:20).

10. **What are the things He has commanded us to do?** To share the gospel and win the lost, and this privilege and responsibility we are to teach new converts to do. "The task of evangelism is not finished until the evangelized (the saved) becomes an evangelist" (a soul winner himself).

11. **The word "go" is a simple word which all should understand, but most professing believers have misspelled it like this:** attend, give, pray, teach, sing, visit, preach, write, read, seminars, Bible studies, CD's, travel, etc.

12. **Will God hold us accountable for obeying the Great Commission?** Absolutely – Ezek. 33:7-8

13. **Suppose you faithfully share the gospel with the lost and they refuse to receive Christ, will God "free you from their blood" in the judgment?** Yes – Ezek. 33:8.

14. **What person in the New Testament testified that he was "innocent from the blood of all men?** Paul See Acts 20:26.

15. **Why has Jesus delayed His coming?** To give us more time to win the lost. (2 Peter 3:9-11)

16. **Does one need to be highly educated to be a soul-winner?** Absolutely not – There was only one college graduate among the Disciples, Judas Iscariot.

17. **Who was perhaps the greatest soul-winner in the Bible?** Andrew

18. **What was perhaps the most significant conversion in history next to that of Paul?** D. L. Moody

19. **List the basic qualifications of an effective soul-winner:**
    a. He must be saved himself – Luke 6:39.
    b. He must love Jesus above everything else – John 21:15-17.

c. He must be empowered with the Holy Spirit – Acts 1:8.

d. He must pray for lost souls. Thus he needs a "soul" book.

e. He must internalize the Word.

f. He must focus on specific lost individuals.

g. He must be willing to take time to show the lost from the Bible three truths:

(1) His predicament – lostness and separation from a Holy God.

(2) God's provision in Christ

(3) How the lost must respond

23. How is MMM carrying out the "World Mission of Christ"?

(1) Stressing the 4th "I".

(2) Participation in Mission efforts abroad in Ecuador, Africa, E-3 led by Tom Jaski, Russia, India and others.

(3) Linkage with Alpha International Ministries of India of which the President of MMM is Chairman of the Board of Trustees.

(4) Making Disciples in the manner of Jesus

(5) The School of Evangelism as a part of MMM.

How To Keep The Great Commission From Becoming Your Great Omission

Some years ago an avid believer in missions wrote a strong article, encouraging Christians to obey the Great Commission. Then he turned it over to the printers, and to his outrage when he read the printed article, he noted that the printer had left the letter "C" off the word "Commission," making it read "Great Omission." So rather than promoting obedience to the Great Commission, the article recommended that Christians "Omit" the Great Commission.

When I read this article, I said to myself, "Modern Day Christians have done just that – they have 'Omitted the Great Commission.' " Statistics show that only 5% of Baptists ever seek to win the lost to Christ and only 1% succeed. Last year, about 10,000 or more of our 43,000 SBC churches did not baptize one person – almost one out of four churches. What a tragedy and yet how easy it is for the "Great Commission" to become your "Great Omission." How can you and I prevent this? If we would avoid this terrible sin, we must take four positive actions:

1. **PRAY – You and I must pray regularly for the world mission of Christ.**

    (1) We should pray that we ourselves would have a heart for the lost. Naturally we are turned inwardly and focused on self, family, close friends. Only the Holy Spirit can change your heart from this selfish state.

    (2) Pray that the Holy Spirit will fill and refresh your life. Jesus told His first disciples not to leave Jerusalem until they were endued with the power of the Holy Spirit, and then He later said, "When the Holy Spirit is come upon you…you shall receive power" (Acts 1:8). In the book of Acts we see the early Christians witnessing across the earth boldly and successfully. The disciples were waiting for the Holy Spirit, for Pentecost had not come; today Pentecost waits for us. You, if you are a Christian, you have the Holy Spirit, but does the Holy Spirit have you?

    (3) Pray for the missionaries already on the fields of the world. Paul prayed for many he did not know, so can we.

    (4) Pray that the Lord of the harvest will send out others – Matt. 9:37-38. When you do, you may be the answer to your own prayers.

    (5) Pray that missions will be a vital part of the DNA of your local church.

2. **PARTICIPATE – Personally in Sharing the Gospel** according to your opportunities. Assuming you are saved and have prayed and depending on the Holy Spirit, take these practical steps:

    (1) Entertain the idea that God may be calling you to serve on some mission field. "No one has the right to hear the gospel twice until everyone has heard it once." Jesus commanded that we pray that the Lord of the harvest would send out laborers – Matt. 9:38. If anyone prays this prayer sincerely, many will find themselves being thrust out.

    (2) If your children or grandchildren feel a call to the mission field, please encourage them to do so.

    (3) Become a member of a Bible class where you can cultivate lost persons.

(4) Select a visiting partner

(5) Sanctify time each week to witness.

(6) Visit the mission field to see a lost world with your own eyes.

(7) Train your heart to be soul minded.

(8) Buy up your opportunities to witness (Ephes 4:15).

(9) SLAY your excuses for not witnessing:

   (a) "I don't have time" – You make time for the important things.

   (b) "I don't know how" – Train and visit with experienced partner.

   (c) "Witnessing is the job of the pastor" – See Acts 8:4.

   (d) "Already busy in the church" – Be sure you're doing 'the work of the Lord' – 1 Cor. 15:58.

   (e) "Let the dead bury the dead."

3. **PAY** – God gives us our directions in 1 Cor. 16:2. Paul is taking a missionary offering, and he gives specific words:

   (1) Give on the first day of the week (Sunday) – give as an act of worship and give regularly.

   (2) Everyone – every believer is to give "According as God has prospered."

4. **PROMISE – God's Promise**

   (a) To the Church – Be assured I am with you.

   (b) To the Individual – Phil. 4:19 – to individuals who support those who go and give their lives.

Chapter 5

Interrelating with others to share your life

Christ must be received individually, but He must be shared corporately with our brothers if we would grow into the likeness of Christ. In fact, we never find the word "saint" in the New Testament, but only the word "saints." As John Wesley said, "There is no such thing as a solitary Christian in the New Testament."

But how does our relationship to other Christians contribute to our own spiritual life and being conformed to the image of Christ? Simply because God Himself has created us as inter-dependent or "members one of another." (Ephesians 4:25; Romans 14:7). How do we show this inter-dependence or how can one believer contribute to the life of another brother or sister?

1. By meeting together for mutual encouragement. Thus God commands in Hebrews 10:25. The word "encouraging" is the Greek word *Parakaleo*, meaning "come alongside" to help another. Jesus Himself calls the Holy Spirit, the *Parakeletos,* the One who comes alongside of each believer to be his Comforter, Teacher, Helper, etc. However, the way the Holy Spirit accomplishes this wonderful ministry is often by sending believers through whom He works.

2. By ministering to others by the use of our spiritual gifts. Thus the Apostle Peter writes, "As every one has received a gift (the charisma), even so minister the same one to another, as good stewards of the manifold grace of God." (1 Peter 4:10). What an amazing statement – that God gives each individual gifts, not for him to use for himself but for fellow Christians by which he ministers all kinds of graces to them. Example: I think God has given me the gift of preaching and teaching. But these gifts are not for me, but for my brothers and sisters. When I share them with others, they are greatly blessed, and not only so, but I myself feel greatly fulfilled and made more and more like Christ. Suppose I fail to share my gifts: I lose them. One wise writer wrote, "When you fail to share Christ with others, you lose Him in your own heart."

3. By mentoring others through spiritual partnerships. Every Christian needs a person who will meet with him regularly and hold him accountable for the way he is living. Such a mentor should love his partner so much that he will not just enjoy a "coffee-drinking" relationship, but will ask the tough questions:

    a. Are you having a meaningful time with the Lord each day?

    b. Are you Internalizing the Word of God constantly?

    c. How are you loving your wife as Christ loved the church?

    d. Are you guilty of internet adultery?

    Illus.: A young college student confided in me that he was being tempted to sin sexually, whereupon he shared his problem with his godly roommate, whose counsel kept him from doing so.

4. By intercessory prayer. There is nothing one Christian can do for another brother as important as intercessory prayer. Intercessory prayer was not a vital part of my praying in my earlier years, but today it has become the heart of all my praying. What a joy and what a privilege. In fact when I find it hard to pray, I begin to intercede and the Holy Spirit comes upon me in a wonderful way.

    I have often said, "When we work, we work; but when we pray, God works." I witness this truth frequently in the lives of those for whom I intercede. Example: I have one grandson, who at the age of 12 was very rebellious and was almost becoming incorrigible. I talked to him often, sent him emails, showed my love in a hundred ways, but I saw no change in his life. Then suddenly God told me to stop talking and working, to lay him upon the altar, and begin interceding for him. I did precisely that and within a few months God began to work in him, turned him around completely and today he is an exemplary young man.

    So in conclusion I am confident in saying that "You can do more than pray after you have prayed, but you can never do more than pray until after you have prayed." How true, how true, and in no area is it more true than when we pray for one another. And at the same time we are praying for others, we are becoming more and more like Christ, conforming to His image, and developing into a true Christ follower.

Collateral Material For The Fifth "I"

When The Bible Does Not Speak – What Then?
Romans 14 And 15

God commands that Christians relate to fellow believers so they can minister to their needs. But how can this be when there is serious disagreement over certain practices and especially when the Bible does not specifically permit or forbid certain activities. As someone observed, "where you find two church members, you have three votes."

The problem of disagreement among believers is not new. In fact, it raised its ugly head in the great church at Rome. The Holy Spirit had brought together a remarkably heterogeneous group of Jewish and Gentile Christians. Paul divided the church into two parties, calling the law-observing Jews "the weak," and the liberated Gentiles "the strong." The "weak party" would not eat meat which had been offered to idols, and the "strong party" saw no evil. The solution to this problem could have been to form two churches, "The Church of the Carnivores," or meat eaters, and "The First Church of the Vegetarians." But Paul did not do this, because he knew the church should be one in the midst of their differences over matters which were neither moral nor immoral but amoral. At this point we must realize that there are some things which are always right and always wrong and thus non-negotiable. Such things are summarized in the 10 Commandments. Having stated this let us now note how Paul tells us to deal with "the negotiables." So Paul tells the Romans how to handle their troubling difficulties in Romans 14 and 15:

I. First, the members of the Church must *Respect* the differences of their fellow members. "Receive one who is weak in the faith, but not to disputes over doubtful things. For one believes he may eat all things, but he who is weak eats only vegetables. Let not him who eats despise him who does not eat, and let not him who does not eat judge him who eats; for God has received him" (Romans 14:1-3). The one who is weak is not weak in his Christian faith, but he is weak in believing he can not eat meat offered to idols. The "strong" are not stronger Christians, but they have a strong faith to believe they can eat meat. So Paul calls on each group to accept one another, for all had been accepted by God. Now Christians aren't divided today over eating meat and vegetables, but I know of several issues which divide Christians today:

a. Going to the theater

b. Wearing make-up

c. Tobacco

d. Card playing

e. Dancing

f. Wearing shorts

g. Music

h. Bible translations

i. Sports

j. Television

k. Alcohol

Leslie Flynn wrote a whole book on *Great Church Fights* in which he says, "Wide disagreements exist today in our churches over certain practices. A Christian from the South may be repelled by a swimming party for both men and women, then offend his Northern brother by lightning up a cigarette. At an international conclave for missionaries, a woman from the Orient could not wear sandals with a clear conscience. A Christian from western Canada thought it worldly for a Christian acquaintance to wear a wedding ring, and a woman from Europe thought it almost immoral for a wife not to wear a ring that signaled her status. A man from Denmark was pained to even watch British Bible school students play football, while the British students shrank from his pipe smoking."[29]

---

[29] Leslie Flynn, Quoted in R. Kent Hughes, *Romans,* Wheaton, Illinois, Crossway Books, 1991, p. 259.

II. Members must *Realize* that members with opposing views on non-essentials can both be perfectly right with God. "One person esteems one day above another; another esteems every day alike. Let each be fully convinced in his own mind. He who observes the day, observes it to the Lord; and he who does not observe the day, to the Lord he does not observe it. He who eats, eats to the Lord, for he gives God thanks; and he who does not eat, to the Lord he does not eat, and gives God thanks" (Romans 14:5-6).

"This controversy over days probably involved Sabbath observance. The Christian Jews' conscience demanded that they observe it. The Christian Gentiles' conscience argued that every day is equally devoted to the service of God. Paul's advice to both is simply, 'Each one should be fully convinced in his own mind.' Each believer is to use his or her powers of reasoning which have at least begun to be renewed by the gospel under the authority of God's Word and act accordingly. The same is to be true of eating and abstaining from meat. The evidence that both the "weak" and the "strong" have right hearts is that they both give "thanks" to God. That is, both do what they do with the intention of serving the Lord."[30]

Illus.: Two of the mightiest preachers of England in the 19th century were Charles Spurgeon and Joseph Parker. Early in their ministries they were close friends and even changed pulpits. Then they had a disagreement. Spurgeon accused Parker of being unspiritual because he attended the theater, and Parker condemned Spurgeon because he smoked cigars. Spurgeon argued that he did not smoke to excess, but when asked what he meant, he said, "No more than two at a time." Who was right? Perhaps neither. Certainly these preachers were not justified in condemning each other. However, if the Holy Spirit convicts you that something is wrong in your life, you had better not do it, even if other Christians are doing it. In my humble (but accurate) opinion, I believe attending most movies and smoking are sins, and I cannot participate in either. But I must not condemn my brother who may disagree.

III. Each member of the church should *Recognize* that one day he will give an account of himself to the Lord Jesus Christ. "But why do

---

[30] R.Kent Hughes, Ibid. pp. 262-163,

you judge your brother? Or why do you show contempt for your brother? For we shall all stand before the judgment seat of Christ. For it is written:

"As I live, says the LORD,
Every knee shall bow to Me,
And every tongue shall confess to God."
So then each of us shall give account of himself to God" (Romans 14:10-12).

The apostle Paul is simply saying this: "Stop trying to be God to one another." You "weak," why do you pass judgment on your brother? You "strong" why do you look down with contempt on your brother? Remember each of us will stand before the judgment seat of Christ (the Bema). Your works will be judged there, especially your motives. Paul graphically describes the scene in 1 Cor. 3:13-15, "Each one's work will become clear; for the Day will declare it, because it will be revealed by fire; and the fire will test each one's work, of what sort it is. If anyone's work which he has built on it endures, he will receive a reward. If anyone's work is burned, he will suffer loss; but he himself will be saved, yet so as through fire."

Realizing the differences that believers were bound to have on matters not clearly forbidden in the Bible, St. Augustine coined a helpful motto which I have endeavored to follow in my churches: "In essentials, unity; in non-essentials, liberty; in all things, charity."

There is room in Christ's church whether you use my translation or not, whether you attend the movies or not, whether you walk to church or ride in your Mercedes, whether you wear wingtips or sandals, whether you sing hymns or chorus, whether you powder your nose or not, whether you watch television or abstain.

The hardest church fight I ever heard about was a conflict over which side of the church the piano should be stationed.

I read of a father and son who parted forever over the color of a boat. Here goes the story. The two were discussing great events of the past – about the years in Little League, hunting expeditions, swimming together, etc. The son said to his dad, "Dad, do you remember the time we were on the lake in that green boat?" His father said, "You are mistaken. The boat was blue, son." The son said, "No, it was green." Again the father said "You are mistaken, it was blue." "Green." "Blue." "Green." "Blue." And his son departed, and never returned.

Some things just don't matter. May we have the patience and humility to allow the Holy Spirit to give the wisdom to see what is essential and what is not.

Lest some one take my above observations to think that there are no fixed standards in the Christian life, I want to make it crystal clear that I am not promoting a damnable heresy. Some have thought Paul was infinitely flexible when he says, "I have become all things to all men that if by any means I may win some." (1 Cor. 9:22). Wrong, wrong. Paul would never say, "I am free to do anything I want." Paul is under "Christ's law." To say "to the thief I became a thief to win the thief; to the drunkard, "I became a drunkard to win the drunkard" is nonsense and a total misrepresentation of what Paul is saying. One person said to me, "I love our pastor because he just lets down his hair, gets on the floor and acts like the rest of us, including drinking a bottle of beer." Pastors or anyone who lives just "to fit in" cannot win anyone. As D. A. Carson says, "They hold to nothing stable or solid enough to win others to it." (The Cross and Christian Ministry, pp. 120-121).

Taking Care of "One Another" – According to God's Word

1. Love one another. John 13:34-45

2. Be devoted to one another. Romans 12:10

3. Give preference to one another. Romans 12:10

4. Don't judge one another. Romans 14:13

5. Build up one another. Romans 14:19

6. Accept one another. Romans 15:7

7. Serve one another. Galatians 5: 13

8. Carry each other's burdens. Galatians 6:2

9. Forgive each other. Ephesians 4:32

10. Encourage one another. Hebrews 3:13

11. Pray for one another. James 5:16

12. Offer hospitality to one another. 1 Peter 4:9

13. Be kind to one another. 1 Thessalonians 5:15

"Kindness makes a person attractive. If you would win the world, melt it, do not hammer it." Alexander Maclaren.

Chapter 6

Investing One's Money Redemptively, beginning with the tithe to one's local church –

Malachi 3:8-10 and 2 Corinthians 9:6-11

Someone said, "The universal passport to happiness on this earth is money." This statement is true up to a point, but not unless one invest his money in redemptive purposes. If one should do so, he must view and use money according to the ten principles laid down in God's Word:

1. God is the Owner of all material things, including money – Haggai 2:8; Psalm 24:1.

2. God has given us all the money and material things that we possess – 1 Cor. 4:7b.

3. We own nothing – Acts 4:32.

4. We are stewards of all God has given us, not owners.

5. We must give an account one day to God as to how we have used our material gifts.

6. If we give as God has commanded, beginning with the tithe to our local church, God will bless us above measure – Mal. 3:10; Luke 6:38 – meaning that we will have what we need when we need (our need, not our greed) – Phil. 4:19.

7. Our giving must be from our hearts, prompted by the grace of God, not because of "compulsion or of necessity" – 2 Cor. 9:7.

8. Because of our grace living, God's grace will enrich us morally and spiritually on this earth so that we grow in Christian character – 2 Cor. 9:7; Luke 15:12.

9. We will experience financial freedom which is essential for abundant living in this life – Mal. 3:10; 2 Cor. 9:7,11.

10. When we get to heaven we will be welcomed by those who were won to Christ because of our giving – Luke 15:9.

Now the question arises, how can we apply the above principles in a practical way? The answer is: By earning and managing our money for the redemption of human kind and the glory of God.

The Bible teaches that God has five fundamental laws on how to make and use our money. Before naming these laws, permit me to summarize the viewpoint of Jesus Christ on money.

Did you know Jesus said more about money than on any other subject? In fact one third of His teaching concerned material matters. Why? Jesus' answer is the most enlightening word in the Bible about money when He stated, "He that is faithful in that which is least is faithful in that which is much" (Luke16:10). Jesus makes the point that that which is least is money and that which is much is spiritual things.

In simple English, Jesus is saying "Money is very important because it is a test—God's test of a person's spiritual relationship to God." In fact, Jesus declares that if a person is faithful in managing his money he will be faithful in spiritual things and if unfaithful in money, he is unfaithful in spiritual things. Furthermore, He asserts that if one is unfaithful in the use of mammon (money) God cannot trust him with spiritual riches. The result of course, is spiritual disaster. Therefore, I appeal to you, "Manage your money God's way or money will murder you spiritually." But how should we manage money?

The Bible teaches that God has five laws for successful money management:

LAW # I – Secure your money righteously. Money is "filthy lucre." No, money is neither moral nor immoral. But it becomes tainted if earned immorally.

- Money should not be earned in violation of your character.

- Money should not be earned when it injures other persons. For example, cheating, selling drugs, alcohol, or the lottery.

- Money should not be earned to the neglect of family, church, and devotion.

- Money should not be earned to fulfill your greed, but your need.

- Money should not be earned by crooked investments.

- Money should not be earned by the desecration of the Lord's Day.

88

LAW # 2 – Save your money *realistically*.

- Don't spend all you make. Save some for the inevitable uncertainties of the future. The wisdom of Solomon says, "Go to the ant, you sluggard! Consider her ways and be wise, which, having no captain, overseer or ruler, provides her supplies in the summer, and gathers her food in the harvest" (Prov. 6:6-8}.

- Save 10% of what you make for unexpected and emergency needs.

But do not hoard your money. Invest your money in souls for heavenly reward or in the judgment your money will "eat your flesh like fire" (James 5:3). This means that your failure to use your riches for God and others will cause you the keenest remorse. When your eyes see the cruelty of your selfishness and greed (costly jewelry, elegant clothing, extravagant homes, high-priced cars, and huge bank accounts) it will be a hellish experience. James 5:1-5 says, "Come now, you rich, weep and howl for your miseries that are coming upon you! Your riches are corrupted, and your garments are moth-eaten. Your gold and silver are corroded, and their corrosion will be a witness against you and will eat your flesh like fire. You have heaped up treasure in the last days. Indeed the wages of the laborers who mowed your fields, which you kept back by fraud, cry out; and the cries of the reapers have reached the ears of the Lord of Sabbath. You have lived on the earth in pleasure and luxury; you have fattened your hearts as in a day of slaughter."

LAW # 3 – Spend your money *responsibly*. You are as responsible for the 90 % as the 10 %.

- Stay out of debt.
- Do not engage in credit buying.
- Do plastic surgery, "cut up your credit cards."
- Avoid impulse buying.
- Avoid ego spending.
- Live within your income.
- Remember, you can buy all kinds of things on credit, but none of it is yours until you pay for it. Purchasing something, when you know you can't pay for it, is stealing.

- Be guided by this economic principle: "If your outgo exceeds your income, your upkeep will be your downfall."

LAW # 4 – Share your money *redemptively*. Jesus said, "Do not lay up for yourselves treasures on earth, where moth and rust destroy and where thieves break in and steal, but lay up for yourselves treasures in heaven, where neither moth nor rust destroys and where thieves do not break in and steal." (Matthew 6:19- 20). How can you lay up treasures on earth? We do this by spending our money on things which are going to heaven. Stocks, bonds, and money are not going to heaven—only redeemed souls. How can we get souls into heaven?

- Start with the tithe. The tithe is 10% off the top given to God weekly through the storehouse, that is, the local church to pay the expenses of the churches incurred in winning the lost (Malachi 3:10; 1 Corinthians 16:2; and Leviticus 27:30).

- Give "as God has prospered you" (1Corinthians 16:2). Everyone is commanded to tithe (Malachi 3:10, Matthew 23:23), but many should give more. You rob God in offerings as well as tithes (Malachi 3:8) if you do not give "as God has prospered."

- Especially invest in areas of direct missions. For example, Mentoring Men for the Master has a goal to train 10,000 pastors and laymen in America. Alpha Ministries, Int'l., has a goal to train 100,000 pastors in India. Ministries which are making an impact for the kingdom of God are worthy of your support.

- Pay your way to the mission field.

LAW # 5 – Send your money *before you*. You can't take it with you, but you can send it on before you. How? You can send it before you by using your money to get people into heaven. This is precisely what Jesus commands us to do and promises an incredible reward in heaven for those who do. Jesus said, "I say unto you, make friends for yourself by the use of your unrighteous mammon so that when you check out, they will welcome you into everlasting habitations." (Luke. 16:9). This is the teaching of our Lord. By the wise investment of material possessions, we can have part in the eternal blessing of men and women. We can make sure that when we arrive at the gates of heaven, there will be a "welcoming committee" of those who were saved through our sacrificial giving and prayers. These people will thank us, saying, "It was you who made it possible for me to be here."

Conclusion

I can say all that I have said above in one statement: God is measuring you and me by the way we *secure* our money, the way we *save* our money, the way we *spend* our money, the way we *share* our money, and the way we are *sending* our money ahead.

- Are you securing your money *righteously*?
- Are you saving your money *realistically*?
- Are you spending your money *responsibly*?
- Are you sharing your money *redemptively*?
- Are you sending your money *before you*?

Collateral Material For The 6th "I"

Give Until You Giggle
2 Cor. 9:6-8, 11

Our motive in giving is vitally important. Our motive in giving should come from the heart, and the motive in the heart must please God. The finest passage on right giving in the Bible is found in 2 Cor. 9:6-11. In this section, Paul describes 4 kinds of givers – *Bad* Givers, *Sad* Givers, *Mad* Givers, and *Glad* Givers.

1. **Bad** givers give sparingly or nothing. Such givers give out of selfishness if they give at all. Such giving is not acceptable to God – 2 Cor. 9:6.

2. **Sad** givers give grudgingly. Such giving is done "grudgingly," not freely, and is also not acceptable to God – 2 Cor. 9:7a.

3. **Mad** givers give "of necessity." Such giving is not acceptable with God, for the giver does not give because he desires to give but he gives only because he feels he has to give – 2 Cor. 9:7b.

4. **Glad** givers. Such giving is highly acceptable and praised of the Lord, because such givers give from their heart – a heart freed from sin and selfishness and a heart in love with Jesus Christ and the gospel. Jokingly I have often said "God loves a cheerful or hilarious giver, but He will take from a "tight wad." Not really. No gift is acceptable to God unless the giver is motivated by love for God and man, and he is able freely to give with great joy and thanksgiving, all the time praying that he can give more and more.

Illustration: Adrian Rogers used to say, "In the event you can give freely and joyously at church, you ought to go home and "giggle" all night long." Often we hear the words, "give until it hurts." Wrong. God's way of giving is to give until it does not hurt but brings great joy to the heart and positive glory to the God who gives to us that we might give to Him and others.

What blessings flow into the lives of the "Glad or Hilarious Givers?" Paul answers in 2 Cor. 9:8, "God is able to make all grace abound to you that you having all sufficiency in all things may abound unto every good work." Then Paul spells out the blessing in even greater detail in 2 Cor. 9:11, "You will be made rich in every way so that you can be generous on every occasion, and through us your generosity will result in thanksgiving to God."

Caution: God does not promise to make us rich materially if we are a glad giver, but He does promise to give us what we need when we need it. Such is the promise of Phil. 4:19, "My God shall supply all your need according to His riches in glory by Christ Jesus." This promise is only for glad givers, as were the Philippian Christians.

Concrete ways to invest your money redemptively:

*   Tithe through a Great Commission local church. "That there may be meat in mine house" (Mal. 3:10).

*   Give generous offerings to support foreign and home missions.

    a. Lottie Moon at Christmas (IMB)

    b. Annie Armstrong (NAMB).

*   Pay expenses on short term missions – (STM)

- Give to special ministries which are training people to win the lost – For example, AIM (Alpha International Ministries) has a goal of training 100,000 church planters by 2020.

- Help missionaries get their education.

- Provide home for missionaries on furlough.

- Purchase equipment for missionaries.

The Christian's Response To Our Economic Crisis
Habakkuk 3:17-19

The floundering economy has caused many Americans to be concerned about the future. The economists are convinced that some form of economic Armageddon looms just over the horizon. But what should be the response of the people of God? A question every Christian should be asking is: could God be using these uncertain times as a wake-up call to see where our trust really lies? Dr. Paul Brewster, whom I have mentored for years, writes that "many American Christians are far more concerned about the collapse of their investment portfolios than about the spiritual collapse of the nation, and that while secular economists see certain doom just around the corner, God's people should view our economic distress as a *blessing in disguise.*"

Let us, therefore, consider some biblical principles which should guide Christians during these uncertain days:

1. **Recognize** that God is sovereign over the economic situation – Psalm 103:19 "The LORD has established His throne in heaven. And His kingdom rules over all."

2. **Realize** that God has a redemptive purpose in allowing the economic crisis:

   (a) to expose corruption not just of Fannie and Freddie but of Tom, Dick and Harry.

   (b) to wake up a sleeping and Laodicean church – Revelation 3:16-17, "So then, because you are lukewarm, and neither cold nor

93

hot, I will vomit you out of My mouth. Because you say, 'I am rich, have become wealthy, and have need of nothing'—and do not know that you are wretched, miserable, poor, blind, and naked."

(c) to show a nation that you cannot serve God and mammon – Matthew 6:24 "No one can serve two masters; for either he will hate the one and love the other, or else he will be loyal to the one and despise the other. You cannot serve God and mammon."

(d) to get the attention of the lost.

3. **Repent** of our personal greed (coveting) which has become the American idol – Col. 3:5, "Therefore put to death your members which are on the earth: fornication, uncleanness, passion, evil desire, and covetousness, which is idolatry."

4. **Relieve** our suffering brothers and ministries if possible – 1 John 3:17, "But whoever has this world's goods, and sees his brother in need, and shuts up his heart from him, how does the love of God abide in him?."

5. **Rejoice** in the God of our salvation when the economic situation is bleak. "Although the fig tree shall not blossom, neither shall fruit be in the vines; the labour of the olive shall fail, and the fields shall yield no meat; the flock shall be cut off from the fold, and there shall be no herd in the stalls: Yet I will rejoice in the LORD, I will joy in the God of my salvation. The LORD God is my strength, and he will make my feet like hinds' feet, and he will make me to walk upon mine high places" (Habbakuh 3:17-21).

6. **Resort** to practical steps to address your economic problems:

   a. Learn to be content – Heb. 13:5; Phil. 4:11.

   b. Pay your bills faithfully.

   c. Prioritize your debt, making sure you don't compromise your home or transportation.

   d. Negotiate with your creditors as needed. Make payment arrangements with your creditors rather than waiting until you miss payments and they come flocking for you.

   e. Downsize if it puts you in a better cash position.

f. Pay extra whenever you can to accelerate your payoff dates.

g. Have a garage sale to generate extra cash to pay down debt or to increase savings.

h. Capitalize on your most valuable assets, your family.

i. Learn to garden, use fresh vegetables and fruit when in season, try a new recipe."[31]

j. If guilty, quit robbing God. Tithe – Mal. 3:10; 2 Cor. 9:6-11.

k. Revisit your spending habits and cut out the ridiculous and unnecessary. Examples:

• Americans spent $21.3 billion on pets in 2002 (twice the amount given to foreign missions}

• $224 billion on eating out

• $67 billion on frozen dinners

• $15 billion on junk food snacks

• $25 billion on gardening

• $22.1 billion on hunting

• $191 billion on personal watercraft

"Where your treasure is, there your heart will be also" – Matthew 6:21.

a. Invest all you can in ministries which change lives and save souls – Luke 16:9

b. Undergo plastic surgery and live within your means, for if your outgo exceeds your income, your upkeep will be your downfall. (The average American has 9 credit cards).

c. Be generous in giving and leave the consequences with God. I have followed this rule in the worse of economic times and have experienced miracle, after miracle, after miracle. Praise the Lord!

---

[31] Crown Finance.com

Chapter 7

The 7[h] "I"

Identification with, support of and service in a local church

Just as the family is indispensable in God's plan for the human race, so is the church for God's people. In our day the church has fallen on evil days, and even some sincere people have said, "Jesus, Yes, but the church, No." But those who would make such a statement do not know or understand what God says about the church and its necessary place in His plan to redeem the world. Of course, many local churches and some pastors have failed miserably and become the "laughing stock" of the media and the world. But this must not be the opinion of those of us who know our Bible and would follow its instruction regarding the church. So let us take note of the biblical description of the church.

1. The church is the "body of Christ." The church is a "body of baptized believers," but it is far more. The church is the creation of God through the new birth, the baptism of the Holy Spirit, and the bestowal of spiritual gifts.

2. The church belongs to Jesus. Jesus categorically defined the church as, "My church." "Upon this rock, I will build my church" – Matthew 16:18. We know that often people think of the church they attend as "my church," and it is good to have devotion to our church, but let us never forget that the church belongs to none other than Jesus Christ.

3. Jesus and the church are not exactly the same, but they are inseparable. Proof of this statement is this fact: Paul persecuted the church severely, and when Jesus encountered Paul on the road to Damascus, Jesus asked him the question, "Saul, Saul, why do you persecute me?"(Acts 9:5), when in fact from Jesus' standpoint, to attack His church was the same as attacking Him.

4. The church is the only institution on earth that will exist forever. Even the family and government shall cease in eternity. But Jesus said, "The gates of Hades (death) shall not prevail against the church" – Matthew 16:18.

5. So precious is the church in the sight of God that for one to "defile" it would be to bring destruction upon his soul. "If any man destroys the temple of God (the local church in this context), God will destroy him, for the temple of God is holy, and that is what you are" – 1 Cor. 3:17.

6. The church is not our Savior, only Jesus is, but the church is the University of Christ, designed by God to "make disciples" of all nations and then to teach them how to be true Christ-followers – Matthew 28:19-20.

7. The church is the only institution on this earth to whom He entrusted the Great Commission of our Lord Jesus Christ. Many Para-church organizations perform valuable ministries in the world, such as the Billy Graham Evangelism Association, Mentoring Men for the Master, Int'l., Campus Crusade for Christ, etc, but none of these can take the place of the church. In fact I have never known a Para-church group to be blessed by God who did not honor the local church. Billy Graham has always stressed the indispensable place of the local churches in his evangelistic ministry, and I make it very clear that MMM is not a church and is devoted to strengthening the local church and helping the pastors who shepherd the flocks of churches.

Of course, there are many more details we need to know about the church than we have covered above. I hope all your questions concerning the church are answered in my treatment to follow:

Church Membership

Salvation is the most important gift you will ever receive. In it, you find new life. Baptism is an important step of obedience because through it you openly, publicly, and unashamedly identify yourself with the new life. Yet, after salvation and baptism, there is still much more that God wants you to have. He wants you to incorporate your new life into His church, the collective body of believers. This is accomplished by uniting with the fellowship and work of a local church.

What is the church?

The Greek word for church, used in the New Testament, is *ekklesia,* which means "the called out ones" or "the assembly." The word is used in the New Testament in two ways. First, it is used to speak of individual local congregations (1 Cor. 1:2). Second, it is used to speak of all Christians in the world who form the church universal (Matthew 16:18).

The universal church, or the whole of all saved people, is the body which you joined automatically when you got saved. You became a member of God's family. You were baptized into this body by the Holy Spirit (1 Cor. 12:13). All Christians everywhere instantly became your brothers and sisters in Christ Jesus. Isn't that great? Welcome to the family!

Now, you need to join a local church family. Of course, this is a decision which you must make as it pertains to which church and which denomination. If you are to grow as a Christian, you must involve yourself in a local church. For your growth as a Christian, church membership is not an option.

Why Join a Church?

As a Christian – especially if you are a new Christian – you have many needs. God established the church to meet the basic needs you have. This section will tell you some of the reasons why you need the church.

First, you need fellowship with other Christians (1 John 1:3). A saved person needs the encouragement and companionship of others who are also Christians. To deny yourself of Christian fellowship is to suffer spiritually. It is hard to grow in the world unless you have a church where you can have a positive Christian fellowship and influence.

Second, you need to identify publicly with the family of God (Acts 2:41-42). By joining and attending a church, you are telling those around you that you are a Christian and a disciple of the Lord Jesus. It serves as a witness and an example to others. It allows them to see who you are and what Christ has done for you.

Third, you need the worship experiences that the church provides. One of the purposes of the church is to worship God through music, praise, petition, and preaching. The church is unique in that it offers this unique opportunity in one setting.

Fourth, you need the church because of its education ministry. The church offers many opportunities to learn the Bible, how to grow as Christians, and many other things which pertain to the Christian life. You can learn from the wealth of knowledge possessed by many mature and wise Christian people.

Fifth, you need the opportunities of services that the church provides. As a Christian, you will never be totally satisfied until you are serving God to your fullest potential. In the church, you can serve by being a soul winner, choir member, teacher, usher, prayer partner, deacon or a host of other things.

Sixth, you need the ministry that a church provides. In your life, you will face many times of crises. You need a group of people who will support you, pray for you, and encourage you. Also, you need the constant ministry of being loved and genuinely cared for. The church provides these things as does no other institution.

Seventh, you need the spiritual direction that the pastor provides. The pastor is a man who is called by God to lead a church and its people. He will help bring spiritual direction to your life and instruct you through his ministry of teaching and preaching the Word of God. He will serve as a counselor and as a special friend.

Eighth, you need the special place for your family that the church provides. The church is a place where you can bring your entire family and find special ministries for each member. The church is capable of ministering to infants, toddlers, children, youth, singles, and adults of all ages. It provides a place where you can be together, grow together, and worship God together.

Ninth, you need the recreation a church provides. Your church will offer activities such as sports leagues, picnics, banquets, special trips, and many others. It is a place where you can enjoy quality recreation with fine Christian friends.

Tenth, the church provides you with the necessary resources to share your faith. It gives you a place to bring your lost friends to hear the wonderful gospel. The church can train you to witness to others through special outreach programs.

Eleventh, and finally, the church gives you a place to give your tithes and offerings which will be used to spread the gospel in your city and across the world.

How do you join a church?

There are a number of ways to join a local church. Most denominations use the following ways of accepting new members. However, these may not be true for every church. After finding a church you want to join, you will want to ask one of its ministers how it receives new members.

First, you may become a part of a local church by professing your faith in Jesus and being baptized (Acts 2:41, 47).

Second, you may join by statement of faith. This means you have already made a profession of faith and have been baptized in another church of like faith and order.

Third, you may join by transferring your letter from another church. This simply means the church which you are presently a member will remove you from its rolls and recommend you to be enrolled into the membership of the other church.

How to find the right church.

This is a very important decision. Finding the right church isn't always easy and may take some searching; but pay the price. It will take time and prayer, but the right church is out there for you. Most of them may not be quite right, but certainly there is one that will meet your needs. You should use the following criteria in finding a new church.

First, does the church believe and preach the Bible? You may be surprised to hear that many do not. They may use the Bible and yet deny its significance. Many churches place tradition and experience above the Bible or equal to it. Beware, because this is not a good practice. The Bible is the authoritative word about God, the Christian life, and other things which pertain to the spiritual and the eternal. The Bible was inspired by God for our instruction and must be preached and taught in the church (2 Peter 1:20-21; 2 Timothy 3:16).

101

Secondly, does the pastor of the church fulfill his role adequately? The pastor should genuinely love the people and seek to be the shepherd of that local flock. He must place himself under the direct authority of God and lead the church as God instructs him. He should practice what he preaches and be a man who is above reproach. He should be a godly man who is able to lead you to Christian maturity. But, there is one word of warning. Do not look for a perfect man. There is no perfect pastor, and to search for one is as hopeless as the search for a perfect church. Yet, there is a pastor who is just right for you.

Third, does the church have a vision to grow and reach lost souls for Christ? Our Lord gave us the Great Commission (Matthew 28:18-20), but unfortunately, many churches are failing to obey Him. You need to find an evangelistic church which is ever seeking to find the lost and win them to a saving knowledge of Jesus Christ.

Fourth, does the church have a good program for educating you and your family in the faith? A church is a place to grow as a Christian. You should be part of a church which can instruct you and mature you in your Christian walk. The church should have a good Sunday School or small groups with classes for everyone in your family, as well as other educational ministries.

Fifth, does the church have special ministries for you? A church should be able to provide evangelism training, prayer meetings, special programs on the home and finances, social occasions and other ministries for your enjoyment and enrichment.

Sixth, does the church provide you with opportunities to serve? You need a church in which you are not only receiving ministry, but also doing ministry. A church that is doing much of anything will have a job for you. Make sure you can become actively involved in the ministry of the church.

Seventh, does the church have a "Vision" – a Divine Blueprint – under which it is marching. Remember Proverbs 29:18 says, "Where there is no vision, the people perish."

These guidelines will help you, but they are in no way exhaustive. You may have some expectations and qualification of your own. Make sure you take a good look at the church and pray for God's wisdom and leadership. Don't seek a church to satisfy your selfishness. Find a church, first of all, where you can serve the Lord, and you will find a church that will serve you. Be assured that the right church is God's provision for your spiritual growth.

By all means, join a church.

Collaterial Material For The 7ᵗʰ "I"

Every Member A Minister
1 Cor. 12:7; 1 Peter 4:10

I read that Napoleon looking at a map of China said, "There lies a sleeping giant. If China ever wakes up, it will be unstoppable."

I submit to you that the Church today is a sleeping giant, for the pews of the average church are filled with people who are doing nothing with their faith except "keeping it." Do you know what we consider an active church member to be?

1. One who attends some.

2. One who gives some money.

But the Bible says a member is active when he is performing a place of service in the church. Illus.: Mr. Gallup took a recent poll which revealed only 10% of church members serve in their church, and 50% said they don't want to serve. "I don't feel <u>led</u>. They have another kind of led – LEAD. They have LEAD in their pants, says Rick Warren.

On the other hand Mr. Gallup took a poll which revealed that 40% of church members say they want to serve if they knew where and how.

I say to you: The church will never be stronger than the core of its lay members and the church is built on *The Nine Pillars Of Lay Ministry*:

1. **PILLAR #1 – Every Believer is a Minister.**

    (a) Ephesians 2:10 says we were CREATED anew to serve.

    (b) 2 Timothy 1:9 says we are saved to serve

    (c) Matthew 28:18 says we are empowered to serve.

    (d) Acts 1:8 says we are empowered to serve

2. **PILLAR #2 – Every Member is Indispensable to the Body.** No "little people" or insignificant ministry. Some ministries are more visible and some are behind the scenes, but all are indispensable to the body. Example: A 79 year old member climbed up many stairs to visit with me in my study. I was thrilled to see this wonderful man. I said, "I've been missing you." He replied, "Pastor, I haven't missed. I have been serving in the nursery." I thanked him most sincerely and profusely. Example: A member with bad health said to me, "Pastor, I'm not able to attend church and help you. All I can do is pray." I replied, "That's the greatest service anyone can render."

   "The most important light in the house is not the chandelier in the dining room, but the little night light in my bedroom which keeps me from stubbing my toe when I get up at night. **It's More Valuable Than The "Show Off" Lights.**" (Rick Warren)

3. **PILLAR # 3 – Every Believer is Gifted for Some Place of Service.** 1 Peter 4:10; 1 Cor.12:7 – Everyone is given a gift for the common good. Illus.: "I don't have a gift, I was behind the door when the gifts were passed out." No, to be a child of God is to be a gifted child of God. The absence of natural abilities does not disqualify you from serving God acceptably, and the abundance of ability does not qualify you to serve.

4. **PILLAR # 4 – No One on This Earth Can Take Your Place.** You have a place in your church and no one else can do it for you. Illus.: I cannot be a W.A. Criswell or Billy Graham, but I am the best and only specimen of Bill Bennett this world has ever seen. God made me to serve in my place. He made me and redeemed me to make a difference, and I intend to do this until God retires me which will be when I expire. Illus.: In 1 Cor 12, Paul say just as every part of your physical body is required to make your body function, it takes every member of the church body to make it function. Humor: R. G. Lee said if the average car had as many missing parts as the average church, it wouldn't go down hill.

5. **PILLAR # 5 – The Way to Find Your Place Is Not Primarily to Know Your Gift, but to Start Serving Somewhere.** Experiment with the different ministries, and God will soon show you where you should be permanently. Illus.: Make yourself useable and the Lord will wear you out.

6. **PILLAR # 6 – You Are Never More Like Jesus Than When You Serve** – Matthew 20:28; Phil. 2:5-9.

7. **PILLAR # 7 – Every Believer Will Give an Account of His Service at The Judgment Seat of Christ** – 2 Cor. 5:10; 1 Cor. 3:11-15; Rev. 22:12.

8. **PILLAR # 8 – Each Believer Will Be Held Accountable Not Only For What He Did But What He Could Have Done** – Luke 12:48.

9. **PILLAR # 9 – The Reward for the Faithful Will Be Absolutely Glorious** because Jesus will say to them, "Well done thy good and faithful servant. You have been faithful over a few things, I will make you ruler over many. Enter thou into the joy of the Lord" (Matthew 25:23).

Chapter 8

Intense Devotion to One's Family, Especially One's Spouse

The family was the first institution established by God on earth – even preceding the government and the church. I am confident that the family was instituted first because it is first in importance in bringing human life into existence and then nurturing that life to become what a holy and loving God intended it to be – to conform to the image of Christ (Romans 8:29) in character and conduct. God began the home by instituting marriage between one man and one woman and pronouncing them to be "one flesh" in a relationship to be ended only by death (Genesis 2:24-25). God did not leave the home without a government to assure its continuance and welfare. The husband was ordained as the head of the home and the wife was to complement him in that role. Later with the coming of the Son of God, Jesus Christ, to this earth, marriage and the family were recognized as paramount in God's plan for His people. Jesus reiterated the same rule set forth by His Father in the Garden of Eden when He said, "For this cause (of marriage) a man shall leave his father and mother and cleave to his wife, and the two shall become one flesh. Consequently, they are no more two but one flesh. What therefore what God has joined together, let no man separate" (Matthew 19:5-6, NASB).

The Apostle Paul underscored the mutual responsibilities of both the wife and husband in his last word to the church in the Ephesians epistle, Ephesians 5: 22-31. "Wives, submit to your own husbands, as to the Lord. For the husband is head of the wife, as also Christ is head of the church; and He is the Savior of the body. Therefore, just as the church is subject to Christ, so let the wives be to their own husbands in everything. Husbands, love your wives, just as Christ also loved the church and gave Himself for her, that He might sanctify and cleanse her with the washing of water by the word, that He might present her to Himself a glorious church, not having spot or wrinkle or any such thing, but that she should be holy and without blemish. So husbands ought to love their own wives as their own bodies; he who loves his wife loves himself. For no one ever hated his own flesh, but nourishes and cherishes it, just as the Lord does the church. For we are members of His body, of His flesh and of His bones. For this reason a man shall leave his father and mother and be joined to his wife, and the two shall become one flesh."

In the light of the centrality of the home and its indispensable place in the plan of God for the human race, what role should the husband play in the home:

1. He should assume the role of being the head of the wife and home (Ephesians 5:23).

2. He should realize that next to God his obligations to his home is the most important call upon his life.

3. He should heed the admonition of the Lord "not to provoke his children to anger; but to bring them up in the nurture and admonition of the Lord" (Ephesians 6:4).

4. While certainly not ignoring his children, the husband should make his wife his first love even before his children.

5. The husband's love for his wife should know no limits but should be as sacrificial as was Christ's love for the church, expressed in the cogent words of the Apostle Paul, "Husbands, love your wives, just as Christ loved the church and gave Himself (in death on the cross) for her" (Ephesians 5:25).

6. Moreover, the husband should know that the spiritual welfare of his wife was also his responsibility, as expressed by Paul "that he might sanctify her" through his example, and teaching (Ephesians 5:27).

7. In a word, the husband should "mentor" his wife even as he has been mentored in our mentoring schools.

To discharge his responsibility to his wife, the husband must become a life-long student of his wife so he will know her needs and how to meet those needs. Such is the specific command of God through the Apostle Peter in 1 Peter 3:7, "You husbands likewise live with your wives in an understanding way, as with a weaker vessel, since she is a woman; and grant her honor as a fellow-heir of the grace of life, so that your prayers may not be hindered." (NASB) Just how can a husband "understand his wife" as commanded by God? I trust the following words will answer this question:

Be A Lifelong Student Of Your Wife And Minister To Her Needs
1 Peter 3:7

Men, how are you treating your bride? The most important aspect of a man's life, except his relationship to Jesus, is the way he treats his wife. In fact no man's life is completely right if things are not right at home. Moreover, for a husband to treat his wife right, he must be a lifelong student of his wife in order to understand her needs and how he can meet those needs. To do the above, a husband must die to self and become Christ-like. In doing so, he may discover that he himself is his wife's chief problem.

A great man of God and friend of mine, Rev. Ray Gilder, Bivocational Ministries Specialist, revealed to me that he asked himself this question for many years, "What is my wife's problem?" One day he discovered that he was the problem. Then God burned a special word in his heart over a period of several months:

"Likewise, husbands, live together according to knowledge, giving honor to the wife as to the weaker vessel, the female, as truly being co-heirs together of the grace of life, not cutting off your prayers" – 1 Peter 3:7 – NKJV.

"Similarly, you husbands should try to understand the wives you live with, honoring them as physically weaker yet equally heirs with you of the grace of life. If you don't do this, you will find it impossible to pray together properly" 1 Peter 3:7 – Philips.

I. Try To Understand The Wives You Live With

Do you know your wife? Have you ever heard her say "you do not understand me?" Refuse to hide behind the false statement, "Nobody can understand a woman." We are commanded by God to "understand the wife you live with." This means *we are to be lifelong students of our wives* – Evaluate Yourself (from 1-10 with 10 being highest) in the Following Areas:

What is it that we need to know?

1. You need to know Her Weaknesses – 1-10 _____

    (a) Does she have a tendency to over commit herself?

    (b) Does she have a problem saying "no"?

    (c) Does she have a tendency to procrastinate?

    (d) Does she get busy and let time slip up on her?

    •   You need to protect her from these.

2. You need to Know Her Strengths – 1-10 _____

    (a) What does she do well?

    (b) What energizes her?

    (c) What gives her a sense of accomplishment?

    •   Encourage her to operate in these areas.

3. You need to know Her Fears – 1-10 _____

    (a) Is she afraid of snakes, spiders, storms, rats, high speed ?

    (b) Never tease or make fun of her fears.

    (c) What makes her feel insecure?

    •   Seek to protect her from and relieve her of her fears.

4. You need to know Her Basic Needs – 1-10 _____

    (a) She needs spiritual leadership. She needs to believe that God is leading you to lead the family.

    (b) She needs affection—Become emotionally sensitive to your wife. She needs a lot of hugs, kisses and "I love yous", not always connected to sex.

    (c) She needs communication. She needs to talk, she needs details. Women speak 25,000 words a day, men speak 12,500 a day. Make sure you save some for her.

110

(d) She needs undivided attention. She needs you to look at her, not the TV or newspaper or a book. She needs you to intelligently respond.

(e) She needs financial support. She needs to know that you will take care of her and the children.

(f) She needs family commitment. She needs to know you are faithful to her and committed to the well-being of the family.

(g) She needs romance and sexual expression. In the Old Testament sexual relations was described as "he knew his wife." Men are interested in their sexual needs. Wives need to know they are really loved.

5. You need to know Her Moods – 1-10 _____

(a) Her chemistry is different from yours. She is subject to mood swings.

(b) Some days even she does not know why she is in a bad mood.

(c) She does not need rejection, correction or a lecture. She needs to be held and loved unconditionally.

At times I have asked my wife, "Honey, what's wrong?" and have preached a whole sermon on this question.

6. You need to know what is Important to Her – 1-10 _____

(a) This means talk a lot.

(b) Encourage her to talk about what she really wants.

7. You need to know Her Ability to Visualize – 1-10 _____

(a) She can see how things will look in advance. Like decorating a home. Men cannot even see it after it is done.

(b) She visualizes a car wreck. If she says "your driving scares me, slowdown."

8. You need to know that She has Built-in Radar – 1-10 _____

(a) She is usually a good judge of character.

111

(b) Listen to her when she warns you about other people. Especially women.

9. You need to know why God made Her Different from You – 1-10
    _____

    (a) He gave her to you to complete you.

    (b) Her strengths and unique traits are to be used to balance your life.

    (c) Actually, you are to blend and balance each other.

10. You need to know Her Love Language – 1 -10_____

    (a) Read Gary Chapman's book—*The Five Love Languages*.

    (b) Decide what your wife's love language is.

    (c) Speak to her in her love language.

11. You need to know Her Past – 1 -10 _____

    (a) What kind of family did she have as a child?

    (b) Did she experience any abuse as a child?

    (c) What traumatic experiences impacted her life?

    (d) Especially know her relationship with her father.

II. **Give Honor To Her**

    How do your honor her?

A. Honor her by placing her above other people and things – 1-10 ____
    ____

    1. Place her above the church—not God, but the church. You are married to her not the church. For the layman, this means placing her above your work. But do not use her or your children as an excuse not to pray, study, or attend important meetings.

    2. Place her above the children—If you do not, when they are gone you will be living with a stranger.

3. Place her above your favorite past time: be it sports on TV, golf, or other hobbies.

4. Place her above your parents—especially your mother. The Bible tells us to leave before we cleave (Genesis 2:24).

B. Honor her by *showing* her she is special – 1 -10 _____

We are to cherish our wives. Genesis 3:16 tells us she is built with a strong desire for your acceptance and appreciation.

C. Honor her by *serving* her – 1-10 _____

Bring her breakfast in bed; give her a foot massage, open doors for her, take her weekly to the beauty parlor.

D. Honor her by *surprising* her with gifts, trips and, outings that she was not expecting – 1-10 _____

This lets her know you have been thinking about her.

E. Honor her by *spending* more on her than she expects – 1-10 _____

She is worth the investment.

F. Honor her by *shielding* her from unnecessary harshness – 1-10 ___

Protect her from crude language, vulgarity, blasphemy. Treat her like a lady and insist others do the same.

G. Honor her by having eyes for her only – 1-10_____

She notices when your eyes follow that shapely young blonde. Burn Job 31:1 in your heart.

H. Honor her by valuing her opinion – 1-10_____. Give her credit for her ideas.

I. Honor her by bragging on her – 1-10_____. Proverbs 31:28 tells us that a godly woman is to be praised by her husband.

J. Honor her by spending time with her – 1-10_____ This proves that you enjoy her presence and highly value her.

K. Honor her by making her your best friend – 1-10 _____. Look forward to sharing you life with her.

L. Honor her as God's precious gift to you – 1-10_____ (Proverbs 18:22).

When you decide to honor your wife, don't tell her you are going to do it, just do it. Let your actions speak for themselves. She has heard too many empty promises that never came true.

A husband can give honor to his wife and still disagree with her. As the spiritual leader in the home, he must sometimes make decisions that are unpopular, but he still can act with courtesy and respect.

III. Become Her Protector

A. Understand what "weaker vessel" means.

    1. It does not mean weaker mentally, spiritually or emotionally.

    2. The word "vessel" refers to an instrument in the hand of God.

    3. She is just as important to God's work as you are.

    4. Weaker refers to her physical strength.

B. God made wives to need protection from dangers, abuse and overwhelming pressure.

C. God designed husbands and fathers to find fulfillment in providing protection for wives and children.

D. This is where the term chivalry comes into the picture. This is one of the characteristics of a knight. Webster describes it as "special courtesy and consideration to women."

E. We should protect our wives from dangerous situations, heavy-duty physical work, physical and verbal abuse and more pressure than they can handle.

F. The husband should treat his wife like an expensive, beautiful, fragile vase, in which is a precious treasure.

IV. Develop A Partnership

A. You are heirs together of the grace of life (1 Peter 3:7).

B. One thing this teaches is that men and women are equal spiritually.

C. The grace of life is the grace given by God to live this life. It is given to you as a team or partnership.

D. Your greatest effectiveness is as a partner with your wife.

E. This should lead you to discover ways to work together.

V. Put Power In Your Prayer Life

A. A key to spiritual power is harmony with your wife (1 Peter 3:7b).

B. A husband's spiritual health depends to a large degree in the way he treats his wife.

C. Discover the power of praying together. There is a tendency to try to act spiritual when conflict arises between you and your wife. We throw ourselves into our work, we pray a lot more and we spend extra time reading the Bible. The Lord's answer is probably like what He told a man who brought a gift to the altar and had problems with a brother. He would say, "Get up and go get things settled with your wife."

Conclusion

Some of you may say, this study has been awfully one sided. My first response would be that this is the typical reaction to any call to dying to self.

Secondly, I am convinced that the man is called to take the lead role in the relationship.

Thirdly, don't use the excuse "I will do my part when she does her part."

Lastly, becoming the husband this verse teaches frees your wife to respond to you properly.

*The above was adapted from Ray Glider's article, "Giving Honor to Your Wife."

In conclusion I am happy and humbled to be able to say that we have seen many husbands grow into godly husbands and fathers through our mentoring emphasis on devotion to the home until quite a few wives have said to me, "Dr. Bennett, I don't know what you are doing to my husband in your Mentoring School, but whatever it is, keep it up; for I have a new husband." Some wives have flatly remarked to me, "Before going to Mentoring School, my husband gave no spiritual leadership in our home, but after attending Mentoring School, he has become our spiritual leader." *Deo Soli Gloria.*

22 Ways to Stay Sexually Pure:

If a husband is to be devoted to his wife, he must first of all be sexually pure. Such purity is more and more difficult because of the sensual and immoral environment which surrounds us today, especially reflected on television, the internet, music, movies, and spoken vulgarities. Thus, I urge you to take all precautions to be sexually pure.

1. **Be sure you are born again, possess a new nature, and have the power of the Holy Spirit on the inside of you, enabling you to overcome sexual lust** (Gal. 5:16). If you are not born again, make an appointment with me or my assistant immediately.

2. **Be convinced that all sex outside of marriage is exceedingly sinful in the sight of God and should not be tolerated at all.** God's command could not be clearer: "Ye shall not commit adultery" (Exodus 20:14; Heb. 13:4). Adultery includes every act of sexual sin as forbidden by this commandment: fornication before marriage, adultery after marriage, homosexuality, lesbianism, incest, child abuse, bestiality, pornography stimulating mental adultery.

3. **Take radical action to prevent mental adultery, which is plain adultery according to Jesus** (Matthew 5:28; 2 Cor. 10:5-6). "Sexual impurity begins in the desires of the heart. Again, Jesus is not saying that lustful desires are identical to lustful deeds, and therefore a person might just as well go ahead and commit adultery. The desire and the deed are not identical, but, spiritually speaking, they are equivalent. The "look" that Jesus mentioned was not a casual glance, but a constant stare with the purpose of lusting. It is possible for a man to glance at a beautiful woman and know that she is beautiful, but not lust after her. The man Jesus described looked at the woman for the purpose of feeding his inner sensual appetites as a substitute for the act. It was not

accidental; it was planned.

How do we get victory? By purifying the desires of the heart (appetite leads to action) and disciplining the actions of the body. Obviously, our Lord is not talking about literal surgery; for this would not solve the problem in the heart. The eye and the hand are usually the two "culprits" when it comes to sexual sins, so they must be disciplined. Jesus said, "Deal immediately and decisively with sin! Don't taper off – cut off!" Spiritual surgery is more important than physical surgery, for the sins of the body can lead to eternal judgment. We think of passages like Colossians 3:5 and Romans 6:13; 12:1-2; 13:14."[32]

4. **Renew your mind by continually internalizing the Word of God** (Romans 12:1-2; Psalm 119:11).

5. **Be absolutely committed to one woman or one man for life.** Humor: It is alleged that after Adam and Eve were married, they were walking in the Garden of Eden, and Eve said to Adam, "Adam, do you really love me?" Adam replied, "Honey, as far as I'm concerned, you are the only woman in the world." You should be able to say this to your wife. I never dated but one girl – Doris. I never wanted to marry but one girl – Doris. I never think of another woman, never compare Doris with another, she is the one and only, now, forever and always.

6. **Make it a rule and never break it under any circumstances:** Never be alone with any woman except your wife (Ephesians 4:27; 1 Thess. 5:22). I had one secretary for 19 ½ years and during all that time I was careful never to be alone with no one else around.

7. **Be careful to guard your eyes and mind.** "The first look is inevitable; the 2nd look is sin" (Billy Graham). Sex begins in the mind. Sex is mental before it becomes physical (Matthew 5:27-28).

---

[32] Warren Wiersbe, *Bible Exposition Commentary,* p.24

8. **Love your wife for who she is today – not when you married her or whom you have wanted her to become.** Remember you married her for "better or for worse" until death do you part.

9. **Do not believe the devil's lie –** "The sexual grass is greener on the other side." 70% of second marriages fail.

10. **Do not make plans to sneak around to enjoy evil.** "Be sure your (sexual) sins will find you out" (Numbers 32:23). Avoid like a plague going to wrong places, seeing wrong people, viewing immoral movies, reading salacious materials, and even talking or joking about immoral sexual activity. "…There must not be even a hint of sexual immorality, or any kind of impurity…nor should there be obscenity, foolish talk, or coarse joking…for this you can be sure: No immoral…person has any inheritance in the kingdom of God" (Ephesians 5:3-5).

11. **Be cleansed from past sexual sins and then do not replay the tapes of past sexual sins** which have been forgiven and removed from you as far as the east is from the west provided you have truly repented and trusted Jesus as Lord and Savior and Him alone (Psalm 103:12; Isaiah 1:18; Phil. 3:13).

12. **Don't Let the Devil Deceive You by The Deception of Gradualism.** Few if any persons plunge into sexual immorality. It is a gradual process consisting of four steps:

    a. **It begins with Distraction** – suppose you are working in an office and suddenly you are distracted by a beautiful woman, and she keeps distracting you for days to follow.

    b. **Attraction – Distraction leads to Attraction.** Now you are attracted to her desk and begin to make sweet comments to her – how nice she looks, how sweet she smells, how beautiful her hair.

    c. **Interaction** – Next, you invite her to eat lunch with you.

d. Finally Interaction leads to Transaction. No longer are you contended to talk to her at her desk, say sweet comments, invite her to lunch. Now you find yourself not with her at lunch but with her in the bed. "You have crossed the Rubicon, and there is no turning back."

13. **Be Certain That You Can't Get Away With Sexual Sin.** Men are deceived in thinking they can keep sexual sin secret. Sexual sin is the most serious sin against God, except the unpardonable sin. Listen to this word from God, "You have sinned **against the Lord; and be sure your sins will find you out**" (Num. 32:23). Illus.: John Doe, my friend and pastor of an enormous church, concealed his sin for 10 years. He was involved with several woman in his church, believing not one of them would divulge it. Then one day one woman squealed, and the whole group came forward. He was forced to resign, and thereafter he founded another church, and another, and another and all failed. He died of a brain tumor at 53 years of age. Just prior to his death, he asked his best friend, "Can I ever be forgiven of such a horrible sin?" My friend replied, "Yes, if you truly repent, but your ministry can never be restored" Read Hebrews 13:4; Prov. 6:32-33.

14. **Do not rationalize any sexual sin but know that all sexual sin is ultimately against a holy God.** Until we see sexual sin this way, we can call it weakness, or what everyone else is doing, but when we see it as offending our holy God and Father, then we can deal with it. Illus.: David sinned sexually and concealed it for one year, after which he cries out "Against thee and against thee only have I committed this sin" (Psalm 51:5). Joseph was hounded for some time by Potiphar's wife to get in bed with her. Finally, he ask her this question, "How can I do this wicked thing and sin against God" (Gen. 39:9).

15. **Remember and never forget this fact:** It is possible for anyone, including yourself, to fall into sexual sin. **Recognize the real possibility of being tempted.** If Jesus, God's Son, could be tempted, that should be clue that you are not bigger than He. Remember 1

119

Cor. 10:12, "Therefore let him who thinks he standeth take heed lest he fall." Remember the advance billing of the Titanic, "Even God couldn't sink it." If you drift into arrogance, not even God can get you through. I have noted that pastors who fell into sexual immorality have often been filled with pride. Read Daniel 4:37.

16. **Know without a doubt, based upon the experience of millions, that sex cannot meet the deepest longings of your heart and soul.** Only God can do this. Listen: "God has made us for himself, and we are restless until we find our rest in Him." The most miserable souls on this planet are those who sought satisfaction in sex only to learn that it does not satisfy. Like drinking salt water, the more you partake, the more you need. Finally, many not finding fulfillment in natural sex revert to all kinds of perversion. In fact our culture today has descended to the depths of pagan immorality. Illus.: Recently a speaker was invited to the UNC Greensboro, to speak on "Anal Sex." I grew up on a farm and observed animals and never saw one sink so low as this.

Let me speak frankly to you men: The body of your wife is yours only in the natural expression of sex, not in using her body to meet your selfish, ungodly desires. Sexual toys, anal sex, oral sex are all abominable and have no place in sexual relations. God commanded us husbands "Husbands, love your wives even as Christ loved the church and gave Himself for us." (Ephesians 5:25). Can you imagine Christ treating the church with ungodly, selfish, vulgar treatment? Perish the thought, and if any of you are guilty, fall before the Lord and ask His mercy and forgiveness before tragedy descends upon you.

17. **Make yourself accountable to somebody, especially in the area of internet pornography.**

    1. Call pornography what it is – adultery
    2. Genuinely repent and receive God's forgiveness
    3. Receive the forgiveness of your wife if possible.
    4. Get a "Big Dog" filtering system and give the code to your wife or some other person.

5. Don't be on the internet in the absence of your wife or late at night.

6. If losing the battle with sexual lust, check out on the website "covenanteyes.com." Recommended by Promise Keepers and Focus on the Family. This program will send your accountability partner every week the sites you have visited.

7. Or get rid of the internet in your home – as Jesus commands "take radical action to avoid physical and mental adultery."

18. **Make friends and associate often with a couple with a strong marriage.** "Do not be misled: bad company corrupts good character" (1 Cor. 15:33). But good company will encourage you in your marriage and convince you that you can have a good marriage yourself. "If you lie down with dogs, you will get up with fleas" (old adage).

19. **Be willing to make the sacrifices necessary to enjoy intimacy with your wife on all levels** – emotional, intellectually, socially, financially, physically. "Husbands, love your wives as Christ loved the church and gave Himself (in death) for her." "If husbands obeyed Ephesians 5:25, the modern feminist movement would collapse in 24 hours," said John Haggai.

20. **Please, please, please don't kid yourself or be a fool and go to hell.** But know this: If you live in sexual sin, you can say "Good Bye" to heaven. The Bible makes it crystal clear that the person living in sexual sin cannot enter God's kingdom but is destined to the "lake of fire" (Rev. 21:8). One may commit an act of adultery, fornication, etc and still be saved. But one cannot practice sexual sin and expect to enter heaven. This fact is set forth in Galatians 5:21; 1 Cor. 6:9; Rev. 21:8.

21. **Be assured that because of God's grace, and through your sacrificial obedience, your marriage can be a "little piece of heaven on earth,"** for that is what God intends. To quote the late Peter Marshall,

"Marriage is the highest hall of human happiness." I beg you, plead and implore you, to make it just that.

22. **Finally, be encouraged by the example of your mentor.** Few people were more unprepared for marriage than myself. My home did not prepare me. My church did not prepare me. My pre-marriage counselors did not prepare me. My church did not prepare me. Duke University and Wake Forest University did not prepare me, even though I took "Marriage and the Family" courses. So to be brutally frank: The first two years of our marriage were rocky. When asked if Doris and I had ever fussed, I replied, "I would not say we ever fussed, but we have had some intense moments of fellowship." But one day I saw that BB was the chief problem in our marriage. I repented and began to live to satisfy Doris not myself. Now – 57 years later – we find ourselves still married and increasingly more happy as our anniversaries roll by. If not already, this can be your experience, too, provided you will die to self, live for Jesus, and the welfare of your spouse. Will you?

Humor:

1. On our 50th anniversary, I asked Doris if she would love me when I'm old and ugly and she replied, "Yes, I do, Bill."

2. On our 57th anniversary, I said to Doris, "Honey, I love you so much that I would like you to remarry me," she replied, " I'll have to pray and think about this first."

Chapter 9

Intentional Discipline of the Physical Body – 1 Cor. 9:27

The Greeks looked upon the physical body as evil and taught that the body would only be delivered from its corruption at death. Even the brilliant Plato embraced this regrettable view of human kind in regarding the physical body. On the other hand, Christianity views the body to be as sacred as the soul and was, therefore, to be "presented to God, as a living sacrifice, holy and acceptable unto God" (Romans 12:1). The body would one day die because of sin (Romans 5:12), but by Christ's resurrection power, it would be raised "a glorious body, even like unto the body of Christ Himself." (Phil. 3:20; 1 Cor. 15:41ff).

If anyone would think the body is evil, he should ask himself the question, "Why would Jesus, the sinless Son of God, have come to this earth and incarnated Himself in a human body like that of man? And why would Jesus have risen from the grave in this same body, glorified, and today sits in heaven in that body at the right hand of God?

There are those who say, "All God requires of us is to keep our souls and spirit in shape and not bother about the body." The Apostle Paul surely kept his soul and spirit in top notch shape, but he asserts that he had to make his body his slave or he would be worthless in the kingdom of God. Listen to his drastic testimony "…I buffet my body and make it my slave, lest possibly, after I have preached to others, I myself should be disqualified." (1 Cor. 9:27).

Permit me to share a testimony regarding the discipline of my body. I disciplined my spirit and soul from the time of my salvation at nine years of age, and 27 years later discovered that my body was deteriorating so greatly that I was feeling very tired and declining in energy and feared I may not be able to continue my ministry. At this point I began to jog three days a week and now daily, until I feel stronger 40 years later and able to work as hard as ever. Where would I be if I had not learned to discipline my body? Perhaps in a rocking chair or even a wheel chair, or maybe in my grave, where many of my peers are. God forbid that I would overstate the place of physical discipline in one's life, but I am compelled to say that physical discipline is as much a part of my life today as is prayer or Bible reading. When I have not been able to jog (very rarely), I am affected psychologically, emotionally, and spiritually. For your soul, body, spirit and ministry, if you do not have a program of physical discipline, begin one now. You'll be glad you did.

The following material enforces the need of physical discipline:

Taking Care Of All Of You – I Cor. 6:19-20; I Cor. 9:26ff

Obesity is now the number two killer in America. Also the number one killer of the children of God. Of all religious groups, Baptists are the fattest! What is the answer to this devastating problem? The discipline of the total person. The Bible speaks clear and loud about "Taking Care of all of You."

I. Taking Care Of Your Body:

Eat Right. Eat in Moderation. If you feel a need to eat till you are full, try this:

- Stock up on raw vegetables. They're filling, nourishing, and they won't put on fat.

- Eat more slowly. Psychologically, if we'd just eat more slowly and wait before taking that second helping, we'd feel better with less. Fast eaters actually consume more than they need because they don't give their bodies time to feel full.

- Don't keep lots of junk food around. If it 's not there, you can't eat it!

- Make a treat a treat. Give yourself a bonus on occasion so that a special treat is really something special. That way it never loses its great taste.

The famous psychologist Dr. Frank Minirth observed: "God never intended food to become a compulsion for any of us. The cycle can be broken, but it must be approached the same way it began, step by step, little by little. Take it a day at a time and you will succeed."

1. Above all, eat breakfast. Why? Researchers have repeatedly proven that breakfast is the most important meal of the day. Why? Because at breakfast – literally "breaking the fast" – we get the nourishment that sustains us through most of the day. What we eat at lunch and dinner really doesn't benefit us until the day is almost over.

2. Get the right amount of sleep. Some people need more; some need less. The key is consistency.

3. Have a physical checkup at least once every two years.

4. Exercise. Choose an exercise routine that fits you and that you can fit in your daily schedule.

5. Flee from sexual sins. "Run away from sexual sin! No other sin so clearly affects the body as this one does. For sexual immorality is a sin against your own body. Or don't you know that your body is the temple of the Holy Spirit, who lives in you and was given to you by God? You do not belong to yourself, for God bought you with a high price. So you must honor God with your body" (I Cor. 6:18-20 TLV). There is a sense in which sexual sin destroys a person like no other, because it is so intimate and entangling, corrupting on the deepest human level. But Paul is probably alluding to venereal disease, prevalent and devastating in his day and today. No sin has greater potential to destroy the body, something a believer should avoid because of the sacredness of the body as affirmed in 1 Cor. 6:19-20.

6. Avoid Internet pornography like a plague.

II. Taking Care Of Yourself Emotionally:

Solomon said "As a man thinketh in his heart, so is he" (Proverbs 23:7). How we think about God, ourselves, others, our lives, yourselves is the key to our behavior.

1. Memorize and Meditate on Scripture

   • It sharpens your mind and concentration.

   • It teaches you to think logically and redemptively.

   • It raises your capacity to learn and stay alert.

- It helps us to combat the lies of the world, the flesh and the devil.

There are multitudes of falsehoods out there from "I'm worthless" to "God can't love me like He loves others" to "some sins just can't be overcome." As we memorize and meditate on Scripture we are exposed to God's truth. Isaiah said God's Word [His truth] never returns void without accomplishing what it was sent out to do(Isaiah 55:11).

2. Learn to love everybody. Through love we reach out, give, share, care, open our hearts to others, become vulnerable, and sacrifice – in fact love makes possible every positive trait of Christian character.

3. Especially love those who won't love you even when you love them. Paul states the Christian approach in 2 Cor. 12:15. "And I will very gladly spend and be spent for you, though the more abundantly I love you, the less I be loved." Every minister must do this.

4. Learn to Laugh. "A merry heart doeth good like a medicine" (Proverbs 17:22). "Laughter is a tranquilizer with no side effects." (Arnold Glasgow)

5. Overcome your fears by letting God love you. "There is no fear in love; perfect love casts out fear" (1 John 4:18). How is this so? When we know the omnipotent God loves us, we realize there is nothing that can overcome us. We may even be killed in this world, but we know we have a permanent home in the next.

6. Learn not to worry. "I have learned in whatsoever state I am therewith to be content (Phil. 4:11). How? Learn to pray, to praise and refuse to entertain worry, think worry, believe worry, tolerate worry, talk worry, write worry "And we know that God causes all things to work together for good to them that love God, to them who are the called according to his purpose" (Romans 8:28).

7. Give everyone, including you, a break. Don't require perfection from your friends, family, your spouse, your children, your boss, your parents, yourself.

8. Give problems time.

9. Watch carefully how you allow yourself to be entertained. TV is the major source of our modern lifestyle. I urge you to assess

your television viewing habits. Are you throwing your life away by watching sitcoms and soaps? A capital "T" followed by a "V" spells victim. Don't become a victim in front of the boob tube.

III. Taking Care Of Yourself Spiritually.

I see a very troubling condition among Christians today: Many are talking about being Christians but are doing little to live like Christians. To such Paul gives this sobering word, "They profess they know God; but in works they deny him, being abominable, and disobedient, and unto every good work reprobate" (Titus 1:16).

A leading Rabbi said some years ago, "We Jews deny Christ by our teaching, but you Christians deny him by your living." Looking Billy Graham in the eye, Mahatma Gandhi allegedly said, "Mr. Graham, I will become a Christian when I see a Christian." What is the trouble? One serious trouble is that the average Christian is prayerless. A recent survey shows he prays only three minutes per day and the average pastor only seven minutes. Another problem is biblical illiteracy. Most Christians don't even know they are to "internalize" the Word, and when most are confronted with this need, they seem to think it is only for the super-spiritual and refuse to do so.

However, I believe the most serious problem among Christians is their failure to understand the seriousness of sin. Most professing believers certainly believe that Jesus Christ paid the penalty for their sins on the cross and they are forgiven. But they to do not believe Jesus broke the power of sin and they do not have to continue to practice and live in sin. Yet Scripture makes it crystal clear that when we came to Christ we were united in His death to sin and made alive to God through Jesus. After stating this truth in Romans 6, verses 1 – 10, Paul then says, "Likewise reckon ye also yourselves to be dead indeed unto sin, but alive unto God through Jesus Christ our Lord. Let not sin therefore reign in your mortal body, that ye should obey it in the lusts thereof. Neither yield ye your members as instruments of unrighteousness unto sin: but yield yourselves unto God, as those that are alive from the dead, and your members as instruments of righteousness unto God. For sin shall not have dominion over you: for ye are not under the law, but under grace" (Romans 6:11-14).

127

The results of thinking we must sin are devastating. Example: The foremost problem in our churches today is the unforgiveness and bitterness of professing Christians toward their fellow Christians. Yet many Christians live in this state, either believing God will understand or that they cannot overcome such an attitude.

So if you would take care of yourself spiritually, you must claim the victory of Christ over all sin in your life. Until you do, you have not taken care of yourself spiritually. How do you do this? You cannot do so alone, so God in His graciousness has given the Holy Spirit to us to enable us to crucify indwelling sin. This glorious truth is stated in Romans 8:13. "For if you live according to the flesh you will die; but if by the Spirit you put to death the deeds of the body, you will live."

Collateral Material For The 9th "I"

The Battle Of The Bulge

Perhaps the bloodiest battle of World War II was called, "The Battle of the Bulge." The allies won this battle on the ground in Germany 65 years ago. But a "Battle of the Bulge" rages as never before in the stomachs of most Americans. Sixty seven percent of Americans are obese, and obesity is the second greatest cause of death in the USA. How can we win this battle over our flesh? After much soul searching, since I am caught in the battle myself, I have concluded from studying God's Word and based upon my experience and research, that there are four stages we can take to win the "Battle of the Bulge" in our stomachs.

I. **Acknowledge Your Present Weight.** 67% of Americans are obese. Obesity is the second or third cause of death in the USA. How about you? As to weight, there are 7 categories into which men fall:

1. Proper weight – consult a scientific chart.

2. Proper weight within 5 pounds, more or less.

3. Under weight.

4. Yo-Yo weight – up and down.

5. Over Weight

6. Heavy Weight

7. Heaven's Gate or Hell awaits.

II. Activate Eight Steps That Will Reduce Your Weight If Needed.

1. Be Honest

2. Admit your present status based on the 7 categories. Don't overlook number 7.

3. Begin to take *drastic* action either to increase your weight if you need to, maintain your weight as it is if you have proper weight, or reduce your weight if you are overweight. Remember the 4 G's of good health: *God, Genes, Grub* and *Gym.* The last two are up to you and are a must if you would possess proper weight. Therefore:

a. Change your eating habits. Consult "A Healthy Nutrition Plan." And read "Taking Care of All of You" on page 122.

b. Chose some kind of physical regimen which fits your temperament and schedule, and engage in it three times a week or more. As to myself I chose jogging or power walking and I will celebrate my 49th exercise anniversary December 2009. My proper weight is 160. I weight 160 but desire to lose 10 pounds in six weeks. My accountability partner is my assistant.

4. Enlist the cooperation of your wife: Her words of encouragement, her cooking, her prayers.

5. Ask your accountability partner to hold you brutally accountable.

6. Do not cease in Shaping Up Your Body, Physically, until you can present it to the Holy Spirit spiritually as commanded in Romans 12:1. Illus: A 13 year old boy on TV weighed 555 pounds. Would he dare present this much "lard" to the Holy Spirit? Of course not. Suppose you are so heavy that you find it hard to get up early to pray? Or to attend vital meetings? Or you have high blood pressure or shortness of breath? Or can't wear your clothes?

Illus: An optimist is the man who picks up his trousers at the cleansers, can't put them on and complains that the "Cleansers are shrinking my pants every time they clean them."

7. Heed this Warning. You will either make your body your slave to yourself, or you will be a slave to your body. This is literally what Paul feared when he wrote 1 Cor. 9:27 which says, "I will treat my body severely and lead it as a slave *(doulagogo)* lest after I have preached to others God will put me on the shelf." Thus keeping our bodies in shape is not just desirable or cosmetic but imperative. It is a shame that of all religious groups, Baptists are the most obese. Do you know of some whom God may have put on the shelf and can use no more? God forbid that it happen to anyone who reads this warning.

III. Accept the Fact That Your Body Belongs to The Holy Spirit and you are to surrender it to Him without reservation (Romans 12:1-2)

IV. Some Food Fun

1. According to scientists, the 2nd day of a diet is the easiest. By that time, you are off of it.

2. The only thing rougher than being on a diet is listening to someone else who is.

3. My favorite food is "Sea Food-All the Food I see."

4. The Agriculture Department says the average American eats 1148 pounds of food a year. Of course, a lot of it goes to <u>waist.</u>

5. Health Rule: Eat like a king for breakfast, A prince for lunch, a pauper for dinner.

6. Recipe from Hippie Cook Book: Cut up lettuce, cucumbers, green peppers, and tomatoes. Add a little marijuana and let the salad toss itself.

7. An apple a day keeps the doctor away, an onion a day keeps everybody away.

8. A chef (not Lee Grossman) is a man with a big enough vocabulary to give the soup a different name every day.

9. An old gentlemen in the hospital refused to eat jello. Pressed for an explanation by the nurse, he replied, "I'm not going to eat anything more nervous than I am."

10. When asked if you have had enough to eat, the educated answer would be "My gastronomic satiety admonishes me that I have reached a state of deglutition consistent with dietetic superfluity."

11. Being diplomatic to the heavy weights: Example – I had a deacon named Howard Leverett, a dear brother indeed, who weighted 400 pounds plus. I used to say to him, "Brother Howard, I need your opinion on such and such a matter, because you carry "more weight" than any member of our church of 3000 members." Example: I baptized a Mrs. Lewey who weighted 400 pounds plus. I weighed about 140 pounds and doubted if I could lift the dear lady out from under the water. So I asked three other guys to assist me, saying to Mrs. Lewey, "Mrs. Lewey, do you realize how important you are?" "No," she replied, and I said, "You are so important that it takes four men to baptize you." I really can't be sure I said these words, but looking back I wish I had.

12. The best way to lose weight is to eat everything you don't like.

13. If you want to know what you ought not to eat, if it tastes good, spit it out.

14. To feel as fit as a "fiddle," you must tune down your middle.

15. A husband who calls his wife the "little woman" very likely hasn't looked lately.

A Healthy Nutrition Plan

There are small things you can do as far as making nutritional choices that can yield BIG RESULTS. Below you will find a nutritional strategy that will help you make smart, tasty choices that will help you shed those stubborn pounds, feel better, look better, and become healthier. This is not about drastically changing your eating habits, but making a few minor substitutions and compromises so that you can still enjoy the foods that you like, but in a healthier way. Open your mind to the possibility of trying different foods and different ways of preparing them.

Some Basic Guidelines

The quantities listed below are the maximum amounts that you should have at one sitting. If you want to eat less than the maximum amounts shown, you're allowed to do that. But don't skip meals! Remember, avoid eating fried foods as much as possible and watch how much salt you eat. Try not to consume more than a teaspoon of salt per day.

Breakfast	Quantity
Eggs	2
Cold Cereal	1.5 cups
Hot Cereal	
Oatmeal	1 cup
Farina	1 cup
Grits	1 cup
Cream of Wheat	1 cup
Pancakes	2 (no more than 5 inches across)
Waffles	2 (no more than 5 inches across)
Yogurt (low fat)	6 oz. (in regular package)

Instructions:

Choose only one of the items above to have for breakfast. Always eat one piece of fruit in the morning. Pay attention to the quantities listed for each item. Don't skip breakfast. Even if you're not hungry, try to at least have a piece of fruit in the morning. You can add berries or sliced fruit to your low-fat or fat-free yogurt and sprinkle it with some granola. The hot cereal should measure only 1 cup AFTER it's cooked. You're allowed to have a small amount of butter (1 pat size) and 2 tbsp of syrup.

More about cereals: The best to eat: Bran, Corn Flakes, Cherrios (plain), Shredded Wheat (not frosted), Total, Puffed Rice, Puffed Wheat, Oatmeal, Farina, Cream of Wheat, Grits.

Avoid: Those cereals that have sugar added to them or have the word frosted in their title.

FRUITS

Instructions:

Fruits are full of powerful vitamins and minerals that can help fight disease and make you feel better as well as increase your energy. Eat as much fruit as you like. There are, however, some fruits that are better than others when trying to lose weight.

Best to eat: Strawberries, blueberries, apples, oranges, cherries, plums, grapefruit, pears, grapes, peaches, cantaloupe, and honeydew melons

Eat less of these: watermelon, pineapple, avocado and those juices that are marked "made from concentrate."

BREADS

The best to eat: whole grain, wheat, whole wheat, multi-grain or Rye Pita Bread.

Avoid: White and sour dough

Instructions:

Breads can be high in something called the Glycemic Index (for more about this, read Extreme Fat Smash Diet). You should limit the amount you consume per day to no more than 2 regular slices.

Milk Products	Quantity
Milk: Skim, 1%, 2%, Fat-free	2 cups
Low-fat Cottage Cheese	3 tbsp.
Yogurt: Low-fat plain yogurt, Low-fat fruited yogurt	12 oz.

Meats	Quantity
Chicken (not fried)	4 oz.
Turkey	4 oz.
Sirloin	4 oz.
Beef	4 oz.
Ham	4 oz.

Instructions:

Meats when eaten in proper quantities are part of a healthy nutritional plan. You should consume no more than two servings of meat in one day. Please pay attention to the quantities that have been listed. 4 oz is approximately the size of one-and-a-half decks of playing cards. Remember, try to limit your fried foods. Grilling, baking, sautéing are healthier ways to prepare your meats and they can be just as tasty!

VEGETABLES/GRAINS

Good to eat: All vegetables except those listed below. Don't fry your veggies. Bake, grill, boil (not too long), sauté, steam. Don't cook with bacon or other fats. Use a small amount—1 tbsp—of butter if you like. Add some spices for flavor.

What to avoid: white rice, white potato (white is the color of the pulp, not the skin. A red-skinned potato is still a white potato, because the pulp is white). Instead, have brown rice and sweet potatoes/yams.

BEVERAGES

Best to drink: natural juices, freshly-squeezed juices, water, flavored water, unsweetened tea, herbal tea, diet soda

Try to avoid or reduce your consumption of: regular soda, alcohol, sweetened drinks, drinks that are marked "made from concentrate."

If you'd like to learn more about a healthy diet or discover tasty, healthy recipes, read Dr. Ian's Extreme Fat Smash Diet or The Fat Smash Diet. They are both available in paperback in bookstores throughout the country or online at www.amazon.com or www.barnesandnoble.com.

10 Smart Swaps that Save Calories

One of the keys to achieving long-term weight loss success is to find ways to continue enjoying your favorite types of foods while you save calories. Whether you're snacking or grabbing lunch on the go, these 10 easy swaps will save calories and satisfy your cravings.

1. In the mood for a crunchy snack? Swap an ounce of Harvest Cheddar Sun Chips for two cups of air-popped popcorn to save 78 calories.

2. Instead of splitting a Chili's Awesome Blossom and sauce with three friends, snack on one medium order of Burger King onion rings to save 357 calories.

3. Swap a cup of strawberry ice cream for a Yoplait Whips, Strawberry Mist flavor, to save 114 calories.

4. Chicken isn't always the best choice when it comes to saving calories. Swap a Wendy's Chicken Club Sandwich for a Jr. Cheeseburger to save 300 calories.

5. Swap a 1.7-oz. package of M&M's Plain Chocolate candies for a half cup of Kozy Shack Real Chocolate pudding to get a chocolate fix while saving almost 100 calories.

6. Wraps sound diet-friendly, but often they are not the best choice. Swap an Au Bon Pain Chicken Caesar Wrap for one 8-oz. low-fat chicken noodle soup to save almost 500 calories.

7. It's not a fiesta for your waistline if you order Applebee's Fiesta Lime Chicken. Swap it for a Tortilla Chicken Melt from the appetizer menu to save a whopping 805 calories.

8. Swap a Wendy's Garden Sensations Southwest Taco Salad for a Garden Sensations Caesar Chicken Salad and save 250 calories.

9. Take your own treat to the mall. Swap one Mrs. Field's semi-sweet chocolate chip cookie for 13 (yes, 13!) Miss Meringue Chocolate Chip Minis to save 170 calories.

10. Chicken is a great salad topper, but fried or crispy chicken ups the fat and calories. For example, at Burger King, if you swap a Tendercrisp Garden Salad for a Tendergrill Garden Salad, you will save 180 calories.

Chapter 10

Instant Repentance and Cleansing from all Sin

When one truly repents and trust Jesus Christ as Lord and Savior, all His sins are forgiven – past, present and future. Not only is that person forgiven, but at the same times he trust Christ and Him alone to forgive and save him from all sins, Christ imputes to him His total righteousness (2 Cor. 5:21). Simultaneously, the Holy Spirit enters the life of that person and imparts to him a new, even "divine nature" (2 Peter 1:4), making him a "new creation" with a new lifestyle (2 Cor. 5:17). Moreover, such a person cannot and will not continue to practice sin because of the "seed of God" which remains within him. "He who is born of God does not practice sin, for the seed of God is in him, and he cannot practice sin because the seed of God remains in him" (1 John 3:9). The Apostle Paul thunders forth this same truth in those convicting words in Romans 6:1 "What shall we say then? Shall we continue in sin that grace may abound? Certainly not! How shall we who died to sin live any longer in it?"

However, the saved, though forgiven and delivered from the practice of sin, may be tempted to sin and even fall into acts of sin. The Apostle John categorically commands God's children in these words, "My little children, these things I write unto you that you sin not," meaning a single act of sin. Then the apostle immediately allows for the possibility of and individual act of sin when he says, "And if any man sin (commits an act, not practice) we have an advocate with the Father, Jesus Christ the righteous" (1 John 2:1-2). Because Jesus is the believer's advocate (attorney) with the Father, the believer's sin is forgiven, provided he will confess his sins. "If we confess our sin, He is faithful and just to forgive us of all our sins and to cleanse us from all unrighteousness." Illus: I read of a pastor who was preaching a series of messages on sin to his people. One of the members said, "I wish you would not preach so much on sin for sin is not serious for Christians as it is for the lost. To which the pastor replied, " Sin is much more serious for the Christian than for the lost, for the Christian knows it is wrong and should not tolerate it." Amen and amen.

Certainly no one can "conform to the image of Christ" unless he keeps his sins "confessed up to date," forsakes them, and is cleansed by the blood of Christ. It is so easy to "cover" our sins, but those who do so shall not prosper, but those who confess and forsake their sins shall find mercy" (Proverbs 28:13). And the promise of God is that if we will walk constantly in the light – in this case the knowledge of constant brokenness and repentance – that "the blood of Jesus Christ His Son will keep on cleansing us from all sin" (1 John 1:7). Illus.: I read that some miners in Kentucky departed from a mine with their faces blackened with soot, except their eyes which were perfectly clean. Why? Because of the flow of the tear glands which protected their eye balls. There is scarcely a greater promise that God gives to His children than that if they will walk in obedience to Him – in instant repentance and cleansing from all sin – a "built in" spiritual gland, the Holy Spirit, will keep applying to their souls the cleansing blood of Jesus. Hallelujah what a Savior!

Since the "instant" repentance from all known sin depends upon our honest and specific confession of same, let us take a "Soul Search through the Scriptures."

Collateral Material For The 10ᵗʰ "I"

Soul Search Through The Scriptures For Cleansing And The Spirit's Infilling

Psalm 139:23-24: "Search me, O God, and know my heart; test my thoughts. Point out anything you find in me that makes you sad, and lead me along the path of everlasting life."

Repentance is necessary for salvation, and for fellowship with god, and revival among God's people. Prayerfully consider the following questions. Every "yes" answer means sin in your life.

In reading these questions, as you are convicted of sin, confess it and repent at once to God. Be willing to make it right. Then you can claim cleansing and forgiveness. I John 1:9, "If we confess our sins, He is faithful and just to forgive us our sins and to cleanse us from all unrighteousness."

Be sure to name your sin to God, as…"Lord, I have not put thee first in my plans." Or, "I have neglected thy Word and prayer." Do not make the least excuse for sin of any kind in your life. Proverbs 28:13, "He that covereth his sins shall not prosper; but whoso confesseth and forsaketh them shall have mercy."

No mater what others do, or do not do, Christian: leave nothing undone on your part. God wants to work through you to bring about a great spiritual awakening. He can begin by your fulfilling every requirement shown by the Lord through the Holy Spirit and His Word. A revival from the Presence of the Lord begins today **if you desire it.** (Read the Scripture first. Ask the question. Give a truthful answer – "yes" or "no.")

1. Matt. 6:14-15

    Is there anyone against whom you hold a grudge? Anyone you haven't forgiven? Anyone you hate? Anyone you do not love? Are there any misunderstandings that you are unwilling to forget? Is there any person against whom you are harboring bitterness, resentment, or jealously? Anyone you dislike to hear praised or well spoken of? Do you allow anything to justify a wrong attitude toward another?

2. Matt. 6:33

    Is there anything in which you have failed to put God first? Have your decisions been made after your own wisdom and desires, rather than seeking and following God's will? Do any of the following, in any way, interfere with your surrender and service to God: Ambition, pleasures, loved ones, friendships, desire for recognition, money, your own plans?

3. Mark 16:15

    Have you failed to seek the lost for Christ? Have you failed to witness consistently with your mouth for the Lord Jesus Christ? Has your life not shown to the lost the Lord Jesus?

4. **John 13:35**

   Are you secretly pleased over the misfortune of another? Are you secretly annoyed over the accomplishments or advancements of another? Are you guilty of any contention or strife? Do you quarrel, argue or engage in heated discussions? Are you a partaker in any divisions, or party spirit? Are there people whom you deliberately slight?

5. **Acts 20:35**

   Have you robbed God by withholding His due of time, talents, and money? Have you given less than a tenth of your income for God's work? Have you failed to support mission work either in prayer or in offerings?

6. **I Cor. 4:2**

   Are you undependable so that you cannot be trusted with responsibilities in the Lord's work? Are you allowing your emotions to be stirred for things of the Lord, but doing nothing about it?

7. **I Cor. 6:19-20**

   Are you in any way careless with your body? Do you fail to care for it as the temple of the Holy Spirit? Are you guilty of intemperance in eating or drinking? Do you have habits, which are dwelling in the body?

8. **I Cor. 10:31**

   Do you take the slightest credit for anything good about you, rather than give all the glory to God? Do you talk of what you have done rather than of what Christ has done? Are your statements mostly about "I"? Are your feelings easily hurt? Have you made a pretense of being something you are not?

9. **Eph. 3:20**

   Are you self-conscious rather than Christ-centered? Do you allow feelings of inferiority to keep you from attempting things you should do in serving others?

10. **Eph. 4:28**

    Do you underpay? Do you do very little where you work? Have you been careless in the payment of your debts? Have you sought to evade payment of debts? Do you waste time? Do you waste time for others?

11. **Eph. 4:31**

    Do you complain? Do you find fault? Do you have a critical attitude towards any person or thing? Are you irritable or cranky? Do you ever carry hidden anger? Do you get angry? Do you become impatient with others? Are you ever harsh or unkind?

12. **Eph. 5:11**

    Do you listen to unedifying radio or TV programs? Do you read unworthy magazines? Do you partake in worldly amusements? Do you find it necessary to seek satisfaction from any questionable source? Are you doing certain things that show that you are not satisfied in the Lord Jesus Christ?

13. **Eph. 5:20**

    Have you neglected to thank Him for all things: the seemingly bad, as well as the good? Have you virtually called God a liar by doubting His Word? Do you worry? Is your spiritual temperature based on your feelings instead of on the facts of God's Word?

14. **Phil. 1:21**

    Are you taken up with the cares of this life? Is your conversation or heart joy over "things" rather than the Lord and His Word? Does anything mean more to you than living for and pleasing Christ?

15. Phil. 2:14

Do you ever by word or deed, seek to hurt someone? Do you gossip? Do you speak unkindly concerning people when they are not present? Do you carry prejudice against true Christians because they are of some different group than yours, or because they do not see everything exactly like you do?

16. Phil. 4:4

Have you neglected to seek to be pleasing to Him in all things? Do you carry any bitterness toward God? Have you complained against Him in any way? Have you been dissatisfied with His provision for you? Is there in your heart any unwillingness to obey God fully? Do you have any reservations as to what you would, or would not do concerning anything that might be His will? Have you disobeyed some direct leading from Him?

17. Col 3:9

Do you engage in empty and unprofitable conversation? Do you ever lie? Do you ever exaggerate? Cheat? Carefully consider – do you overcharge?

18. II Tim. 2:22

Do you have any personal habits that are not pure? Do you allow impure thoughts about the opposite sex to stay in your mind? Do you read that which is impure or suggest unholy things? Do you indulge in any entertainment that is unclean? Are you guilty of the lustful look?

19. Heb. 10:25

Do you stay away from the meetings or preaching the Gospel? Do you whisper or think about things while God's Word is being read or preached? Are you irregular in attendance at services? Do you neglect to attend or participate in meetings for prayer? Have you neglected or slighted daily or private prayer? Have you neglected God's Word?

Do you find the Bible and prayer uninteresting? Have you neglected thanksgiving at meals? Have you neglected family devotions?

20. Heb. 13:17

Do you hesitate to submit to leaders in the church or elsewhere? Are you lazy? Do you rebel at requests given to you in the work of the Gospel? Do you in any way, have a stubborn or unteachable spirit?

21. James 1:27

Have you allowed yourself to become "spotted" by the world? Is your manner of dress pleasing to God? Do you spend beyond what is pleasing to God on anything? Do you neglect to pray about things you buy?

22. James 4:6

Do you feel that you are doing quite well as a Christian? That you are not so bad? That you are good enough? Are you stubborn? Do you insist on your own way? Do you insist on your "rights?"

23. James 4:11

Have you dishonored Him and hindered His work by criticizing His servants? Have you failed to pray regularly for your pastor or other spiritual leaders? Do you find it hard to be corrected? Is there rebellion toward one who wants to restore you? Are you more concerned about what people will think, than what will be pleasing to God?

+ + + + + + + + + + +

If you have been honest and true in the matter of repenting of your sins, then you are ready for God's cleaning. Remember these things:

1. If the sin is against God, repent to God, and make things right with God.

2. If the sin is against another person, repent to God and make things right with the other person.

3. If the sin is against a group, repent to God, and then make it right with the group. *If there is full confession and repentance, there will be full cleansing.* Then the joy of the Lord will follow.[33]

Ten Desperate Steps To Personal Revival

Some years ago a noted theologian said in effect "Revival does not come to nice people but to the desperate." Dr. J. Edwin Orr, the world's foremost authority on revival, was asked by a student, "Dr. Orr, besides praying for revival, what can I do to help to bring it about?" He then replied, "You can let it begin with you."

If it would begin in me or you, you must be desperate for it enough to take the following 10 Desperate Steps to Personal Revival:

1. Get thoroughly dissatisfied with yourself. Complacency is the deadly enemy of spiritual progress. The contended soul is the stagnant soul. Amos 6:1. When speaking of earthly goods Paul could say, "I have learned…to be content"; but when referring to his spiritual life he testified, "I press toward the mark." So stir up the gift of God that is in thee.

2. Set your face like a flint toward a sweeping transformation of your life. Gen. 32:20. Timid experimenters are tagged for failure before they start. We must throw our whole soul into our desire for God. "The kingdom of heaven suffereth violence, and the violent take it by force."

3. Put yourself in the way of the blessing. It is a mistake to look for grace to visit us as a kind of benign magic, or to expect God's help to come as a windfall apart from conditions known and met. There are plainly marked paths which lead straight to the green pastures; let us walk in them. To desire revival, for instance, and at the same time to neglect prayer and devotion is to wish one way and talk another. 2 Chronicles 7:14.

---

[33] Material for Soul Search adapted from one used by Ms. Bertha Smith, long time missionary.

4. Do a thorough job of repenting. Do not hurry to get it over with. Hasty repentance means a shallow spiritual experience and lack of certainty in the whole life. Let godly sorrow do her healing work. Until we allow the consciousness of sin to wound us we will never develop a fear of evil. It is our wretched habit of tolerating sin that keeps us in our half-dead condition. Mt. 3:8; Psa. 57.1

5. Make restitution wherever possible. If you owe a debt, pay it, or at least have a frank understanding with your creditor about your intentions to pay, so your honesty will be above question. If you have quarreled with anyone, go as far as you can in an effort to achieve reconciliation. As fully as possible make the crooked things straight. Mt. 5:23-24.

6. Bring your life into accord with the Sermon on the Mount and such other New Testament Scriptures as are designed to instruct us in the way of righteousness. Titus 2:11-14. An honest man with an open Bible and a pad and pencil is sure to find out what is wrong with him very quickly. I recommend that the self- examination be made on our knees, rising to obey God's commandments as they are revealed to us from the Word. Matt. 5:28; 5:4; 5:23; 5:44; 6:19-25; 7:12; 7:1; 6:33; 5:8; 5:13; 5:14. There is nothing romantic or colorful about this plain downright way of dealing with ourselves, but it gets the work done. Isaac's workmen did not look like heroic figures as they digged in the valley, but they got the wells open, and that was what they had set out to do.

7. Be serious-minded. You can well afford to see fewer comedy shows on TV. Unless you break away from the funny boys, every spiritual impression will continue to be lost to your heart, and that right in our own living room. The people of the world used to go to the movies to escape serious thinking about God and religion. You would not join them there, but you now enjoy spiritual communion with them in your own home. The devil's ideals, moral standards and mental attitudes are being accepted by you without your knowing it. And you wonder why you can make no progress in your Christian life. Your interior climate is not favorable to the growth of spiritual graces. There must be a radical change in your habits or there will not be any permanent improvement in your interior life. I Pet. 5:8

8. Deliberately narrow your interests. The Jack-of-all-trades is the master of none. The Christian life requires that we be specialists. Too many projects use up time and energy without bringing us nearer to God. If you will narrow your interests God will enlarge your heart. Phil. 3:17; Psa. 27:4. "Jesus only" seems to the unconverted man to be the motto of death, but a great company of happy men and women can testify that it became to them a way into a world infinitely wider and richer than anything they had ever known. Christ is the essence of all wisdom, beauty and virtue. To know Him in growing intimacy is to increase in appreciation of all things good and beautiful. The mansions of the heart will become larger when their doors are thrown open to Christ and closed against the world and sin. Try it.

9. Begin to witness. Find something to do for God and your fellow men. Refuse to rust out. Philemon 1:6 Make yourself available to your pastor and do anything you are asked to do. Do not insist upon a place of leadership. Learn to obey. Take the low place until such time as God sees fit to set you in a higher one. Back your new intentions with your money and your gifts, such as they are.

10. Have faith in God. Mark 11:22. Begin to expect. Look up toward the throne where Your Advocate sits at the right hand of God. All heaven is on your side. God will not disappoint you. (Adapted from *Rut, Rot Or Revival* by A. W. Tozer)[34]

---

[34] Stephen F. Olford, Heart-Cry for Revival, quoted A. W. Tozer, Westwood, New Jersey: Fleming H. Revell, Company, pp. 30-31

LaVergne, TN USA
11 December 2009
166735LV00001B/7/P